Editor-in-Chief and Founder:
Lyndon H. LaRouche, Jr.
Editorial Board: *Lyndon H. LaRouche, Jr. , Helga Zepp-LaRouche, Robert Ingraham, Tony Papert, Gerald Rose, Dennis Small, Jeffrey Steinberg, William Wertz*
Co-Editors: *Robert Ingraham, Tony Papert*
Managing Editor: *Nancy Spannaus*
Technology: *Marsha Freeman*
Books: *Katherine Notley*
Ebooks: *Richard Burden*
Graphics: *Alan Yue*
Photos: *Stuart Lewis*
Circulation Manager: *Stanley Ezrol*

INTELLIGENCE DIRECTORS
Counterintelligence: *Jeffrey Steinberg, Michele Steinberg*
Economics: *John Hoefle, Marcia Merry Baker, Paul Gallagher*
History: *Anton Chaitkin*
Ibero-America: *Dennis Small*
Russia and Eastern Europe: *Rachel Douglas*
United States: *Debra Freeman*

INTERNATIONAL BUREAUS
Bogotá: *Miriam Redondo*
Berlin: *Rainer Apel*
Copenhagen: *Tom Gillesberg*
Houston: *Harley Schlanger*
Lima: *Sara Madueño*
Melbourne: *Robert Barwick*
Mexico City: *Gerardo Castilleja Chávez*
New Delhi: *Ramtanu Maitra*
Paris: *Christine Bierre*
Stockholm: *Ulf Sandmark*
United Nations, N.Y.C.: *Leni Rubinstein*
Washington, D.C.: *William Jones*
Wiesbaden: *Göran Haglund*

ON THE WEB
e-mail: eirns@larouchepub.com
www.larouchepub.com
www.executiveintelligencereview.com
www.larouchepub.com/eiw
Webmaster: *John Sigerson*
Assistant Webmaster: *George Hollis*
Editor, Arabic-language edition: *Hussein Askary*

EIR (ISSN 0273-6314) *is published weekly (50 issues), by EIR News Service, Inc., P.O. Box 17390, Washington, D.C. 20041-0390. (703) 777-9451 ext. 415*

European Headquarters: E.I.R. GmbH, Postfach Bahnstrasse 9a, D-65205, Wiesbaden, Germany
Tel: 49-611-73650
Homepage: http://www.eirna.com
e-mail: eirna@eirna.com
Director: Georg Neudecker

Montreal, Canada: 514-461-1557

Denmark: EIR - Danmark, Sankt Knuds Vej 11, basement left, DK-1903 Frederiksberg, Denmark.
Tel.: +45 35 43 60 40, Fax: +45 35 43 87 57. e-mail: eirdk@hotmail.com.

Mexico City: EIR, Sor Juana Inés de la Cruz 242-2 Col. Agricultura C.P. 11360 Delegación M. Hidalgo, México D.F.
Tel. (5525) 5318-2301
eirmexico@gmail.com

Canada Post Publication Sales Agreement #40683579

Postmaster: Send all address changes to *EIR*, P.O. Box 17390, Washington, D.C. 20041-0390.

Signed articles in *EIR* represent the views of the authors, and not necessarily those of the Editorial Board.

The Law of Hamilton and LaRouche Is Natural Law

EIR Contents

www.larouchepub.com Volume 43, Number 44, October 28, 2016

I. Let Us Begin Actual Human History

Germany's Potential Role in Developing the World Land-Bridge

The keynote address of Helga Zepp-LaRouche, founder and chairwoman of the Schiller Institute, to the Schiller Institute conference in Essen, Germany on Oct. 21, 2016.

Dear ladies and gentlemen, honored guests, most honored *chargé d'affaires* [of the Embassy of China in Berlin]: I am very happy that this event has begun with this wonderful performance of Chinese art, because I believe that art is the best way to open the hearts of mankind to new ideas.

We are hosting this conference in Essen—and a similar conference took place just two days ago in Lyon, France, in cooperation with the China Club EM Lyon Forever[1]—because we intend to put on the agenda a new perspective for Europe, namely cooperation between Germany and France on the New Silk Road. By organizing many such conferences, we want to make much better known the political, economic, and cultural potential which exists in the New Silk Road policy. Because the New Silk Road, which is already developing effectively at a very rapid tempo, is fast becoming a project of understanding among nations and is developing into the World Land-Bridge.

EIRNS/Chris Lewis

Helga Zepp-LaRouche

Obviously the New Silk Road provides enormous potential for business "opportunities," that is, business relations, but actually it involves something much more important. It involves not only linking together the world's continents through infrastructure and development corridors, and making innovation the science driver for the world economy with the goal of raising productivity. It involves something very much deeper and more fundamental than that: Can mankind, in the face of all the crises which we see before our eyes, establish a world system in which people can live together in peace? Is humanity capable of defining a higher level of reason, or are we compelled—by keeping to the well-worn paths—to hit a stone wall, perhaps losing civilization forever?

I believe that it is possible to find this higher level of reason, and to make it effective. Just as the ancient Silk Road, during the Han Dynasty some 2,000 years ago, was not only a means for the exchange of goods, but also of technology, culture, and philosophy—and thus led to an enormous improvement in the living standards of all the participating nations and regions—so, I believe, it is possible to put on the agenda today a New Silk Road, a new policy for binding nations together.

---

1. EM is one of France's largest schools for management.

The Seventh Xiangshan Forum, in Beijing Oct. 11-12, convened more than 500 delegates from law enforcement agencies and institutions, and representatives from the expert community from almost 60 countries.

The Existential Threats

But I can not talk about the advantages of this new paradigm without at least very briefly identifying the great dangers which the world is confronting at this moment, and why, in my opinion, the New Silk Road is not an option, but a necessity, if we are to avoid a catastrophe.

Seventy-one years after the end of the war in Europe, what once seemed unthinkable—the possibility of a new great war—is looming. So much so that German Foreign Minister Frank-Walter Steinmeier recently said that he could no longer rule out a direct military confrontation between the United States and Russia. American Vice President Joe Biden said that the United States was planning a cyber-attack on Russia, "at the time of our choosing and under the circumstances that have the greatest impact," because of alleged Russian manipulation of the American election campaign—a statement that Konstantin Korsachov, the chairman of the Foreign Affairs Committee of Russia's Federation Council, has called the greatest threat since the Cuban Missile crisis. Maria Zakharova, spokesperson for the Russian Foreign Ministry, said that the Obama Administration is carrying out a "scorched earth policy in bilateral relations."

And Russian and Chinese military officials at the Seventh Xiangshan Forum in Beijing a week ago warned that the Obama Administration has gone a long way in preparation for a first strike against their two countries on the basis of the Prompt Global Strike doctrine!

Nor can anyone claim that Europe doesn't face other crises. After the Brexit, the future of the European Union (EU) is somewhat unclear. The refugee crisis has shaken Europe's very foundations, and esteem for the EU handling of this crisis has absolutely collapsed internationally, as I myself have had to recognize many times.

We are approaching a new financial crisis like that of 2008, only this time potentially very much worse, of which Deutsche Bank's crisis is only the tip of the iceberg. And everyone knows that if Deutsche Bank, with its 42 trillion euros of outstanding derivatives goes bankrupt, then all the banks which are allegedly "too big to fail," would be immediately affected. And as a former member of the board of a large European bank told me a few days ago: If the storm breaks out and the governments do nothing to bring matters under control, then the biggest losers will be those who have earned their life savings with honest work. We will have a different kind of Europe, full of ungovernability—and chaos and revolution will be at hand.

I point to that as a scenario simply because, if we do not change course, the danger is that we will enter an unprecedented crisis.

China's Meteoric Progress

Now the good news is that, because all these crises are man made, if we change our policies, we can overcome them. Western media have scarcely reported what a dramatic change has occurred over the past three years, since President Xi Jinping put the New Silk Road on the agenda. A totally new perspective has emerged, which has developed with enormous momentum and in which more than 70 nations are already cooperating.

Since the economic reforms of Deng Xiaoping, China itself—as most of you know, either through visits there or reports—has carried out an unbelievable transformation from total underdevelopment to at least partial industrialization. Interestingly, the Chinese economic miracle proceeded according to the same principles as the German Economic Miracle of reconstruction after World War II, namely the principles which were then applied by the *Kreditanstalt für Wie-*

deraufbau, and which were close to the ideas of the German economist Friedrich List, who, interestingly, is the best known and most loved German economist in China.

Over a span of 40 years, China has been able to accomplish the development that took the industrialized nations up to 200 years. China has long since stopped relying on cheap production, but is already the world market leader in many areas such as high-speed rail. By the end of 2015, China had built 20,000 kilometers of high-speed rail. It will have 38,000 kilometers of high-speed rail by 2025, linking all major cities in this way. It has surpassed many western nations in the digitalization of industry and is the market leader in many areas.

Over this period of 40 years, China has freed 700 million people from poverty. I believe there is no country that has done as much for human rights as China, because poverty is the greatest violation of human rights; therefore to have done what China has done is a great contribution to human civilization. China has even published a white paper on overcoming extreme poverty entirely by 2020; only three percent of the population still lives in extreme poverty, and China is determined to change that.

At the recent G-20 summit in Hangzhou, hosted by China, China announced its proposal to base the world economy on innovation and win-win cooperation, and declared China's intention to become an innovative nation by 2020—in my view it already is one—an internationally leading innovative nation by 2030, and a "world powerhouse" by 2050. China declared that innovation is the primary driving force of an economy, and that it is determined to escalate the benefits of scientific and technological progress in all areas—modern agriculture, information technology, protection of the environment, the ocean and space industries, and healthcare and services.

President Xi Jinping has given Chinese scientists the mission to achieve fundamental breakthroughs in four specific domains: the structure of matter, the evo-

Sputnik

Indonesian President Joko Widodo, Chinese President Xi Jinping, Russian President Vladimir Putin, and German Chancellor Angela Merkel arrive for the opening ceremony of the G20 Summit in Hangzhou, China.

lution of the universe, the origin of life, and the nature of conciousness. It perhaps will surprise some, but Chinese economic theories are very close to what we call physical economy as it was developed by Wilhelm von Leibniz, and taken further by Friedrich List; Mathew Carey; Henry C. Carey, Abraham Lincoln's economic adviser; and Wilhelm von Kardorff, Bismarck's chief economic adviser, and to whom we owe Bismarck's shift from supporting the free trade outlook to advocating of physical economics, and Germany was enabled to become an industrial nation.

According to the theory of physical economy—which has been further developed by Lyndon LaRouche, my husband, whom we have here with us—the source of society's wealth does not lie in the control of trade relations (for example, a TPP or TTIP), or in "buying cheap, selling dear," or in the control of raw materials, and certainly not in the derivatives trade and other speculative "products." Society's wealth lies ultimately in the creative potential of the human spirit and the application of scientific and technological progress to the production process, which raises productivity, and thus is the source of the improvement of living standards and life expectancy.

China has developed, along with the nations along the Silk Road, a comprehensive plan for scientific and technological cooperation, and will establish joint research laboratories and centers, and organize technology transfer and the exchange of 150,000 scientific personnel and 5,000 young scientists. The goal is explicitly to raise the productivity in the cooperating countries.

At the G-20 Summit, President Xi Jinping announced that China will share breakthroughs in scientific and technological progress immediately with the developing countries, so that their development is not delayed.

en/kremlin.ru

Russia President Vladimir Putin looks on as Japanese Prime Minister Shinzo Abe and President of the Republic of Korea Park Geun-hye greet each at the Vladivostok Eastern Economic Forum plenary session.

This ideal, to my knowledge, was first proposed in the 15th Century by Cardinal Nicholas of Cusa, who likewise said that human inventions are so important for the human race that they should immediately be placed in an international pool in which all can participate, so that their development will not be held back.

Greatest Construction Program in History

China's Silk Road conception is the greatest infrastructure and industrialization program that has ever existed on Earth. Already there are 30 treaties between China and other nations; 70 nations are cooperating, involving 4.4 billion people altogether. The total investment amounts to $1.4 trillion, which is twelve times greater than the Marshall Plan after the Second World War, measured in today's purchasing power.

The Silk Road is a perspective for the economic transformation of the Earth over the next 30 to 40 years, and by no means involves only trade routes to Europe and Africa. The expression "Silk Road" was coined by the German geologist Ferdinand von Richthofen in 1877, but "Silk Road" is actually a synonym for the integration of regions and routes for the exchange of science and technology, and what the Silk Road technology was then—how to produce silk, how to produce porcelain—is today the most modern technologies, like the question of nuclear fusion, or space technology.

It's obvious that Germany's future lies in coopera-

tion with this project, because Germany has something which is highly valued in the whole world, and that is the German *Mittelstand* (small and medium-sized enterprises), which in fact contributes the most to innovation. Germany, which as you know, has hardly any raw materials, was only able to achieve high productivity and a high living standard because we always had a very high rate of scientific and technological progress, and a very high rate of exports. In Germany it is the *Mittelstand* that is the source of most inventions and patents, that provides 85% of expenditures for the general welfare, and it is the German *Mittelstand* which would profit the most from cooperation with China—not only through direct German investments in China and Chinese direct investments in Germany, but primarily through joint ventures in various projects in third countries.

High-Speed Changes

Over the last six weeks the process of change has reached an enormous rate of speed, and there is now a totally new alignment. At the beginning of September, there was an economic forum in Vladivostok, where China's New Silk Road was integrated with the Eurasian Economic Union under the leadership of Russia. Prime Minister Shinto Abe of Japan was there, as well as South Korea's President Park, both with large economic delegations. Immediately after that, there was the G-20 Summit in Hangzhou, at which China presented a new model for economic relations among nations, focussing on the United Nations Charter, with its emphasis on sovereignty and respect for different economic and social models.

President Xi said on this occasion that the old model is no longer sustainable; we now need an innovation-directed strategy. We will take the lead in science and technology, and conduct the fundamental research needed to solve the scientific and technological problems holding back economic and industrial development. We will speed up the commercialization of research and development, foster strategic emerging sectors, and move industry up to a medium-high level of the value-added chain.

Xinhua/Geng Yuhe

The first train carrying containers departs the logistics terminal jointly built by China and Kazakstan in Lianyungang City, in China's Jiangsu Province, Feb. 25, 2015.

This philosophy was then discussed further at the directly following summit of the ASEAN nations in Laos, a summit which actually consummated a strategic orientation toward China and, for example, adopted the Chinese position on the conflict in the South China Sea. Their final declaration stated that China's development was an opportunity for the entire region. Philippine President Rodrigo Duterte, during his visit to China, has just said that he will now prioritize the relationship with China. The same interests were stressed at the immediately following conference in Goa, India of the BRICS nations—which are at the core of Eurasian integration—and remaining tensions were downplayed. The reason is clear: The Asian dynamic continues to grow.

The tempo of this strategic realignment shows very clearly that the center of world politics has shifted to Asia. When the first train arrived from China five years ago, it created great surprise. But now, 20 trains a week are coming from different economic regions—Zhenjiang, Lianyungang, Harbin, Yiwu, Wuhan, Chengdu, Chongqing—to Duisburg, Hamburg, Rotterdam, Lyon, and Madrid. The Eastern and Central European countries have long since realized the advantages of working with China, because China has invested in the trans-

port corridors that were agreed on in 1994 at the EU Conference in Crete but never realized, because of the Troika's austerity policy. China has expanded the port of Piraeus, or is soon to expand it; it is building the railroad line from Greece to Serbia, towards Hungary; it is connecting the Oder-Elbe-Danube Canal with the other European waterways.

The governments of Greece, Serbia, Hungary, the Czech Republic, Italy, Switzerland, and Portugal have stated that they see the path to the future in cooperation with the Chinese Silk Road.

At the same time, a parallel banking system has developed, the Asian Infrastructure Investment Bank (AIIB). Seventy countries immediately joined as founding members, although the United States put enormous pressure on them not to do so, among them such close allies as Great Britain, Germany, France, Japan, Australia, and Canada. Simultaneously the New Development Bank (NDB) of the BRICS emerged and is now operational, along with the Silk Road Fund, the Maritime Silk Road Fund, the Bank of the Shanghai Cooperation Organization, and also the Contingent Reserve Arrangement to protect countries from speculative attacks.

To all the cities and regions that are cooperating with these projects, it is perfectly clear that it is to their advantage. For example, Duisburg—which was once a steel city but has experienced a great economic slowdown—is now in an upswing, because it is profiting enormously from being the largest inland port on the Silk Road.

China has made Europe an offer to fully cooperate in the industrialization of Africa. And what should prevent us from doing this, along with using this Asian dynamic to develop the Balkans and Southern Europe, which has suffered economic hardship from the Troika's policy? For example, Greece's industry, through the Troika's policy, has shrunk by a third. Everything can be built up again through China and the Silk Road. At the same time, the Middle East must urgently be reconstructed, and naturally, Africa.

Speculators' Propaganda

What should prevent us from taking up these offers? The answer is clear: that some countries—the United States and Great Britain—insist on a unipolar world, although this unipolar world has long since ceased to exist. The danger is that the trans-Atlantic world will fall into the "Thucydides trap"—that it will see the rise of Asia as a geopolitical threat instead of recognizing the opportunity for everyone to participate in win-win cooperation.

The propaganda against the New Silk Road is gigantic. On September 12 the Said Business

Confucius (551-479 B.C.)

School of Oxford University published a report asserting that China's huge investments in infrastructure—the equivalent of $10.8 trillion over the last decade—is leading to an imminent economic collapse of both China and the world. This is obviously a desperate attempt to slander the Silk Road, and the argumentation is that of the typical investment banker—that investments in infrastructure don't yield enough profit.

Chinese officials have already countered this argument, saying that China has a different appraisal of risk than the western rating agencies, and that it sees the potential of a country in its future, while the bankers view the past. In the history of industrialization of every country, with no exception—whether it be Germany, the United States, Russia, or any other country—the development of infrastructure was always the *sine qua non* for its transformation into a modern economy.

The idea that one realizes a profit on infrastructural investments directly, as, for example, by tolls on private highways, is obviously absurd. The profit is in the rise of productivity in the whole nation, and the higher the level of development, the denser the infrastructure network must be. If you then include all forms of infrastructure—energy, water, communications, education, healthcare—then it is totally clear: The higher the density of infrastructure, the higher the productivity, the living standard of the population, and life expectancy.

And the more advanced industry is, all the more relevant is the time factor; thus we absolutely believe that the Transrapid technology remains a technology of the future, and we will hear a lecture on this subject today after lunch.

The Oxford University researchers then let the cat out of the bag as to why they published such a laughable report: They said specifically that the Chinese model should no means become the model for other developing countries, certainly not for Pakistan, Nigeria, or Brazil. That China should not be a model. But all predictions that China will collapse economically are totally absurd; look at the just published figures on annual growth. The Gross National Product is up 6.7%, exactly as predicted; industrial production is up 6.1%—what European country would not rejoice over a 6.1% annual increase? The rise in consumption is 10%. Electricity use is up 4.8%, thanks in no small part to the ongoing electrification of China's western regions.

The stance of these investment bankers against infrastructure is one of the reasons why we in Germany have an infrastructure investment deficit of somewhere around 2 trillion euro—ramshackle bridges, bad roads, and the rest. That is also the reason why the IMF conditionalities of the last 50 years have prevented the infrastructural development of the Third World, and why we today have such a great stream of refugees out of Africa into Europe.

A Cultural Renaissance

There is another false argument, namely that China actually only wants to replace Anglo-American imperialism with Chinese imperialism. I think this is the projection of people who simply cannot imagine that any country today has a positive model for the organization of relationships on this Earth.

In that regard, you must understand that China not only has a 2,500-year-old Confucian tradition, but that there is at present a powerful Renaissance of Confucian thought in China on all

wikipedia

Bui Dam in Ghana, built and financed in large part by China, 2009-2013. Europe, Japan and India, already engaged in Africa, should cooperate with China in the common aim of mankind to industrialize Africa.

levels of society. Part of that thought is, for example, the idea of life-long self-improvement, self-perfection, the idea that each person should become a *junzi*, someone morally self-possessed. To that tradition also belongs the idea of the harmonious development of all nations, and the win-win idea of Xi Jinping conforms precisely to that. It also corresponds—if we in Europe go back in our history—to the ideas of Nicholas of Cusa, who said in the Fifteenth Century that there can only be harmony in the macrocosm if all the microcosms develop harmoniously and to their mutual advantage. There is a deeper affinity between Confucianism and European humanism than most people realize.

The problem isn't China. The problem is that we in Europe have forgotten this tradition, or have shunted it aside—the ideal of humanity that was associated with the Italian Renaissance, the Ecole Polytechnique in France, or the German Classical period. Who today still has the optimistic image of man of Wilhelm von Humboldt, who said that the goal of education should be to create a beautiful character? Who still has the ideas of Friedrich Schiller, who said, Every man has the potential to become a beautiful soul, for whom passion and duty, freedom and necessity, are the same? The only person who can do so is the genius; but Schiller meant that all people have the potential for genius.

That means that we have distanced ourselves from these humanistic ideals, or that they have meaning for only a very small part of the German population. And looking at our youth culture, no one can doubt that it is dominated by a very far-reaching degree of brutalization; ugliness is everywhere, violence is glorified, teachers are afraid of their students. The German Industrial Association wrote several years ago that 25% of 15-year-olds are not employable because they are not interested in anything.

This is the first time in the history of Europe and America that we have apparently accept the idea that the next generation will be worse off than we are. For youth this means that they have no future, no reason to study and to learn.

And it is totally different in China. China's youth have experienced the Chinese economic miracle, and most of them—not all, of course, but most—have an enormously optimistic conception of themselves and their country. That means that also in this respect, Europe and Germany could cooperate with the Silk Road so that our youth can regain a perspective.

Germany is the most important economy in Europe. I think that if we can get Germany to consciously say "yes," officially, to cooperation with the New Silk Road, that would perhaps be the most decisive step which Germany could take for the preservation of world peace.

The Common Aims of Mankind

The issue is a totally new paradigm, a totally new era in the history of mankind. The issue is the idea that mankind as a whole represents a higher order than all of the nations. If we focus on the common aims of mankind, what Xi Jinping calls the "community of destiny" or the "community of the common future of mankind," then, I think, everything is possible.

What are these common aims?

The industrialization of Africa, for example. If Germany and Europe were to cooperate with China, with Japan and India—all of whom are already engaged in Africa—we could create a situation in which tens of thousands of people are no longer either dying of thirst in the desert or drowning in the Mediterranean, while fleeing from war and starvation. We could build up the Near and Middle East again, which is our moral responsibility, because we have tolerated these wars which everyone knows were built on lies.

China's youth have experienced the Chinese economic miracle, and most have an enormously optimistic conception of themselves and their country. Chinese astronaut Wang Yaping teaching a class in Space physics live from orbit to 60 million students, including these Beijing high school students, during a June 2013 Space mission.

We could give all children access to education and thus set free the real creative potential of mankind.

We must concentrate on a new scientific revolution—the principle of life, the creative potential of the human spirit as a physical force in the universe. We must better understand the processes of the Solar system, of the Galaxy, of the Universe as a whole. We must put ourselves in the position of astronauts, cosmonauts, and taikonauts, who all report that when you look down on the Earth from space, it is only a small blue planet, which has no limits, but is also infinitely vulnerable.

We must place ourselves in the position of Krafft Ehricke, the German rocket and space pioneer, who defined three laws of astronautics:

The first law: Under the natural law of this universe, nothing and no one imposes any limitations on man, but he himself.

Second: The rightful field of action for mankind is not only the Earth, but the whole Solar system, and as much of the Universe as he can reach under natural law.

And third: When he expands into the Universe, man fulfills his destiny as an element of life, endowed with the power of reason and the wisdom of the moral law within himself.

The infrastructural development of the New Silk Road therefore means not only the improvement of the landlocked regions of the Earth, but also the improvement of the nearby space environment. The Chinese lunar program, with Chang'e 4 and 5, plans to land space vehicles on the far side of the Moon in two years, with the purpose of later mining Helium 3 for a future fusion economy on Earth, which will finally bring mankind energy and raw material security.

Just now there was a successful docking of the space vehicle Shenzhou-11 with the Tiangong Space Station, where two Chinese taikonauts will carry out experiments for 30 days. China will have a permanent space station in a few years—as early as 2020 or 2022. Thus cooperation in space is one of the most important areas of the common aims of mankind, because it challenges man practically on all fronts of his physical and spiritual existence, and it reflects to the highest degree the independence of the human spirit and absolutely touches the philosophy of his existence. I think that we can survive the challenges with which we are currently confronted on Earth with this orientation to the future, and on the level of reason. But I think we can do it.

Europe Must Dump Geopolitics and Seize The Opportunities of the New Silk Road

Adapted from EIR Strategic Alert Service *No. 43, of* October 27, 2016

The New Silk Road policy initiated three years ago by Chinese President Xi Jinping offers tremendous opportunities for Europe to overcome the several existential crises it faces, and join the overall dynamic for development sweeping over Asia and a majority of underdeveloped countries. That potential, however, is not properly recognized in the trans-Atlantic world, where the strategic realignment underway is usually presented in the media as a danger.

The opportunities for cooperation in the grand design are there to be seized, but Europe has scarcely done so, which is why the Schiller Institute (SI) decided to organize two more conferences on the New Silk Road theme in two crucial cities in Europe: Lyon, in France, which was the historical terminus of the ancient Silk Road, and has just recently become the terminus for the first cargo train from Wuhan travelling on the "Iron Silk Road,"— and Essen, in the Ruhr area of Germany, very near Duisburg, which is the first stop of that same railway, as well as being Europe's largest inland port.

The conference in Lyon, on Oct. 19, was co-organized by the Club China EM Lyon FOREVER, an alumni association of the Lyon Ecole de Management (EM), a prestigious national business school which also runs a campus in Shanghai.

In Essen on Oct. 21, the Schiller Institute was honored to welcome as a speaker the chargé d'affaires of the Chinese Embassy in Berlin, Zhang Junhui, who presented the progress of the New Silk Road and the Chinese government's wish for greater economic cooperation with Germany, both countries being the largest economies on the two ends of the Silk Road.

The conference was opened by Helga Zepp-LaRouche, and also heard later from French presidential candidate Jacques Cheminade of the Schiller Institute, who both stressed that Europe needs to reject imperialism and geopolitics, and that France and Germany should return to the tradition and economic policy of de Gaulle and Adenauer, which put an end to centuries of strife and warfare, by focussing on the mutual benefits of cooperation.

Over the course of the discussion, it became clear that the mission Europe must take up today, is to help

EIRNS/Chris Lewis

From left to right: Professors Reinhart Poplawe and Dieter Ameling, Helga Zepp-LaRouche, Professor Shi Ze, and translator.

Friedrich List   *Henry Carey*

ensure the development of Africa, in combination with China.

Zepp-LaRouche stressed that the German small and middle-sized companies (*Mittelstand*) above all can greatly benefit from cooperation with the One Belt, One Road policy, since these are the enterprises that bring the most innovation into the economy.

Presentations from German experts in technological and industrial/infrastructure fields made clear why Germany must remain an industrial nation, and a leader in the field of science and innovation. The disastrous effects of the deindustrialization policy and lack of investment in infrastructure were underscored.

A Harmony of Interests

In opening the conference in Essen, Helga Zepp-LaRouche presented an overview of the dangers confronting the world today, but also the very real possibility of opting for a completely new paradigm, as originally proposed by President Xi Jinping and endorsed since then by a growing number of countries.

The New Silk Road is the greatest program of industrial and infrastructure development that has ever existed on the planet, she said, and Europe must not miss the chance of being part of it. In fact, the "economic miracle" that China has created in the past 40 years is based on the same principles of physical economy that Germany used in the post-war period to carry out the German economic miracle, and which go back to Alexander Hamilton, Friedrich List, Mathew and Henry Carey, etc.

These principles are reflected in the fact that China

has managed, over the recent period, to lift 700 million people out of poverty. The New Silk Road, Zepp-LaRouche stressed both in Lyon and Essen, is not just a string of isolated transport projects, one after the other, but infrastructure which transforms and raises the platform of the entire national economy of the countries affected, including those in Central Asia which are now landlocked.

Professor Shi Ze of the Chinese Institute for International Studies was a featured speaker in both Lyon and Essen. The New Silk Road, he stressed, is an open and all-inclusive policy which all countries are welcome to join, including all those in Europe. It is no longer just a concept, as first announced by Chinese President Xi Jinping; it is being put into place right now. It is based on the idea of "harmony in diversity," i.e. cooperation among different cultures and civilizations to their "mutual" interest.

Shi, who has closely worked with the SI over the past few years in Europe and in China, heartily thanked the Institute for its efforts to promote the Silk Road policy and a dialogue of cultures.

Cheminade painted a devastating picture of the effects of the EU policy, contrasting it to the approach of the SI. He also called for the rights of all refugees in the EU to be protected.

On the cultural level, Zepp-LaRouche insisted on the convergence of the Confucian tradition in China, which is now being actively revived, with the high points of culture in Europe, as exemplified by Nicholas of Cusa, and on the need to establish multilateral relations on such a level, far from the confrontationist approach that prevails today.

Europe's Mission to Develop Africa

The reality on the ground in Africa and the relevance of China's "One Belt, One Road" policy to Ethiopia and by extension to the entire continent, were presented in Essen by the Ethiopian Consul General in Frankfurt, Mehreteab Mulugeta Haile. He gave a comprehensive overview of the economic development policy, driven by infrastructure, which his country has implemented over the past 25 years, with striking successes.

China has extended crucial assistance to Ethiopia, including in the form of low-interest loans. Thanks to Chinese companies and agreements, the first ever rail-

Mehreteab Mulugeta Haile

Jacques Cheminade

way linking Addis Abeba, the capital of the country, to the port of Djibouti, was opened on Oct. 5, shortening the delivery of Ethiopian maritime imports and exports from seven days to ten hours. This is just the first leg of a nation-wide rail network that is to connect Ethiopia with all of its neighboring countries. Assistance in other infrastructure projects, including power generation, has served not only to develop Ethiopia, but to integrate the economies of the region through increasing connectivity.

Mr. Mehreteab's presentation led to a discussion, in the question-and-answer period, on the role of Europe, together with China, in developing Africa, as the only way to effectively and humanely stop the migration to Europe with its high death rates.

This proposal was put forward concretely by Jacques Cheminade as a task for Germany and France. Helga Zepp-LaRouche added that Italy, whose Prime Minister Renzi has recently endorsed the New Silk Road policy and opposed new sanctions against Russia, should be prominently included in the effort. Shi Ze proposed that, given the lack of any such institutional cooperation for the moment, a new "mechanism" should be developed to facilitate the new orientation.

Mr. Mehreteab fully supported the proposal, and firmly asserted that Africa is no longer interested in "aid" that comes with political strings attached, "in the guise of human rights." Rather, Africa needs capital investments, technology transfers, and investment in infrastructure. "Do not give us the fish," Mr. Mehreteab said, quoting an old saying, "but teach us how to catch the fish." He added that Europe should follow the example of China, which is offering investment, technology transfer, and low interest loans on normal international standards.

The IMF and World Bank, on the contrary, as Zepp-LaRouche pointed out, lend to Third World countries so they can repay their debts to the international banking

en.people.cn

The Ethiopia-Djibouti Railway, constructed with Chinese funding, design, equipment, and operations, shrinks the trip between Addis Ababa and Djibouti from one week to ten hours.

Prof. Reinhart Poprawe

Prof. Dieter Ameling

system, rather than investing the money in projects to ensure economic growth.

Cheminade pointed to the fact that an urgent project is already on the table, which Europe and China could jointly help finance and realize, namely the replenishment of Lake Chad. The most efficient means to do so is through the Transaqua project, diverting a small portion of the waters from the Congo Basin up to Lake Chad (cf. *Strategic Alert Service* 14/16, 48/14). The participants expressed the resolve to act on this proposal in the near future.

Technological Optimism

Participants in Essen were treated to a welcome respite from the anti-technology, anti-industry, "green" ideology that dominates the public arena in Germany. The other four German speakers, in addition to Helga Zepp-LaRouche, addressed how Germany can both contribute to the New Silk Road policy, and benefit from the new paradigm.

Prof. Reinhart Poprawe, Director of the Fraunhofer Institute for Laser Technology at the Technical University of Aachen, who also holds an honorary professorship at Tsinghua University in Beijing, pointed to the fact that China is no longer the producer of cheap goods for the world, but is making very rapid progress in several hi-tech frontier areas where it is climbing to the top and is on a par with Germany, Japan and the United States. Poprawe believes that Germany, with its "Industry 4.0" program, is well-positioned to cooperate with the ambitious "China 2020" program.

Prof. Dieter Ameling, a former president of the German Steel Association who also held top positions at the leading steel companies, presented a perspective of close cooperation in the steel and beneficiated iron sectors between Germany and China, which has now become a much larger producer. But he also warned very starkly, that if the anti-energy policy of the German government prevails, energy-intensive sectors of industry will emigrate to countries where the electricity bill is not kept artificially high because of the so-called renewables policy. Electricity in Germany already costs twice what it does in the United States, and 50% more than in France. He also strongly polemicized against the prevalent view that carbon dioxide emissions are reponsible for climate change.

Prof. Reinhold Meisinger of the Technical University of Nuremberg, who has been a visiting scientist at Tongji University in Shanghai for many years, gave a detailed report on the revolutionary "Transrapid" or maglev-train technology originally developed in Germany, which is being used commercially on the Shanghai-Pudong track, after being scrapped at home. He indication that some of the newly-built high-speed wheel-technology trains are running and will run on tracks that are designed for future use by maglev trains. The energy consumption of a national maglev grid in China would, however, be far too big to be provided by "renewables," which is why China is expanding its nuclear power and hydroelectric sectors. Meisinger reported that his Chinese master students at Tongji University are eager to work actively on developing new maglev systems that will run on Chinese tracks in the future.

The conference was also addressed by Willy Pusch, of a citizens initiative for the construction of a new tunnel system to handle rail freight in the Middle Rhine

CHRISTINE BIERRE

Christine Bierre

Professor Shi Ze

Valley, which is a crucial segment of the Rotterdam-Genoa rail line. The proposed 100 km Westerwald-Taunus tunnel, twice as long as the new Gotthard Tunnel in Switzerland, could handle up to four times more freight than today — and that without the extreme decibels that are presently torturing, particularly at night, the population living in the Rhine Valley between Bonn and Mainz.

De Gaulle and the New Silk Road

As the first speaker of the conference in Lyon, Helga Zepp-LaRouche immediately challenged the audience on the right level: "What would Charles de Gaulle do today to safeguard and protect the French people from the unprecedented dangers in the world, namely the twin threats of potential nuclear confrontation between the United States and Russia, and the immediate possibility of a meltdown of the trans-Atlantic financial system…?"

Since these dangers are the result of human policies, she said, they can be overcome by choosing an entirely different political course. She went on to present LaRouche's four cardinal laws to solve those problems, before going through the development and the prospects of the New Silk Road/World Land-Bridge dynamic, as she did in Essen.

Professor Shi Ze's presentation was similar to that in Essen, but he also stressed how close the partnership between China and France has been, due to the fact that Charles de Gaulle opened diplomatic relations with Beijing ten years before the other advanced countries.

A particular area of interest for China, he pointed out, is setting up joint ventures with France in third countries. He also stressed repeatedly, how important it would be to make joint investments in Africa, in infra-

structure, energy, and transportation, as called for in a Franco-Chinese joint statement signed in 2015.

Christine Bierre, a leader of Solidarité & Progrès, reviewed the status of relations between the two countries. Paradoxically, she said, François Hollande's policies toward China seem much better than those he applies in France! As a privileged ally of China since 1964, thanks to de Gaulle, France is sharing some high technologies with China, in exchange for "accompanying" China's strong development.

Airbus airplanes are being assembled in China, and nuclear power cooperation has been close for 30 years. On June 30, 2015, the two countries signed a statement calling for joint construction of nuclear power stations in third countries, on the model of the Hinkley Point agreement in Great Britain. Strong collaboration has also developed to reduce air, water and soil pollution, which the Chinese have made a priority.

Today, in the spirit of Leibniz's grand Eurasian design of the Seventeenth Century, Christine Bierre proposed to strengthen four other areas of cooperation as well, i.e., space exploration; the development of new generations of nuclear power (fusion, pebble bed reactors, thorium molten-salt fast reactors, and hybrid fission/fusion reactors); modernization of the rail connections; and joint Franco-Chinese projects in Africa. All that requires that France once again adopt a solid industrial policy oriented to the future.

Jean-Christophe Vautrin, president of the Club China EM (Ecole de Management) Lyon FOREVER, which co-sponsored the conference, presented the activities of this club of alumni, which organizes conferences and events dedicated to Chinese economic policy, history, and culture.

A PROGRESS REPORT

China's Belt and Road Initiative Is a Bullet Train

by William Jones

Oct. 21—While the U.S. public has only recently become acquainted with the Chinese Belt and Road Initiative (BRI) because of the almost total neglect of the project by the myopic U.S. media, the BRI has already shown itself to be the most comprehensive development project since the post-war Marshall Plan. But the BRI has already gone far beyond the Marshall Plan in the magnitude of investment and number of countries benefiting from it.

No doubt the initial, hostile reaction to the project on the part of the Obama Administration was based on the hope that China had neither the means nor the will to carry out such a gigantic venture, and that it would soon peter out. It were wrong on both counts. When China took the initiative to build new financial institutions, such as the Asian Infrastructure Investment Bank (AIIB), to help promote the Belt and Road, Obama attempted to strong-arm governments to stay out of it. The net result of his efforts was paltry. Among the largest economies, only Japan still keeps its distance from the AIIB. Like the AIIB, the BRI is alive and well, and growing rapidly.

The prestigious Chongyang Institute for Financial Studies at Renmin University recently published a report on the development of the BRI over the first three years of its existence. The results are astounding.

Transportation Grid for All Eurasia

The initial proposal was to build two major intercontinental thoroughfares, with rail, high-speed rail, telecommunications, electric power transmission lines, energy pipelines, and major industrial projects set up along the way. One route would go across Eurasia, and the other would be a southern route, combining rail and sea transport to India and Africa. Present plans have already broken the bounds of the initial conception.

There are at present six major land routes in various degrees of construction: a Eurasian Landbridge through Kazakhstan and Russia to Europe, and corridors designated as China-Mongolia-Russia, China-Central Asia-West Asia, China-Pakistan, Bangladesh-China-India-

Test run on the Ankara-Istanbul high-speed railway built by the China Railway Construction Corporation, Jan. 4, 2014.

Myanmar, and China-Indochina. In addition, the "21st Century Maritime Silk Road" will have two distinct sea routes, one from China's ports to Europe through the South China Sea and the Indian Ocean, and the other from China's ports through the South China Sea to the South Pacific.

While the project has been initiated by China, it is aimed to benefit all of the nations along the way and is open to *all* countries to participate.

Indeed, President Xi himself has been the key promoter of this project since he initiated it in September 2013 in a speech in Kazakhstan at Nazarbayev University. Since then, the Chinese President has visited 37 countries (eighteen in Asia, nine in Europe, three in Africa, four in Latin America, and three in Oceania) where he has promoted the idea of the Belt and Road and has received a very warm response in all these countries. During his visit to the Middle East earlier this year, it was clear that the project would have a tremendous, beneficial effect on the economies in that war-torn region.

The BRI has also provided the framework for both multilateral and bilateral agreements between China and its neighbors, and has helped to invigorate the activities of the numerous regional associations that have grown up: the Shanghai Cooperation Organization, Eurasian Economic Union, the China-Central Europe Economic Cooperation Organization, ASEAN+China, the Asia-Pacific Economic Cooperation (APEC), Asia-Europe Meeting (ASEM), and others.

Along the Belt and Road, China has signed free trade agreements with 11 countries and bilateral investment agreements with 56. In all, China has signed agreements on Belt and Road policy with most countries in Central Asia and the Caucasus, and has issued joint statements on policy planning for building the Belt and Road with a number of regional or subregional bodies such as the European Union, the 16 Central and East European countries, the Greater Mekong Subregion, and the Africa Union.

The Eurasian Landbridge, the China-Mongolia-Russia Corridor, and the China-Central Asia-West Asia Economic Corridor will chart a path that will bring in-

Xinhua/Pan Chaoyue

The container ship Indian Ocean, *operated by China Shipping Container Lines, at the Gulf of Suez, Egypt, May 18, 2015.*

creased trade and development to the Persian Gulf and the Southwest Asian countries.

The China-Pakistan Economic Corridor, the China-Indochina Peninsula Economic Corridor, and the Bangladesh-China-India-Myanmar Economic Corridor will help extend economic benefits to the countries of South and Southeast Asia and Africa.

Transportation Is Key

Building transportation grids, particularly railroad grids, is absolutely fundamental in creating a development corridor. Along these transportation routes will be built telecommunications networks and power generation and energy grids, transforming them into corridors of development and connectivity.

As of June 30, 2016, 39 freight rail lines between China and Europe were operational, some extending into Africa. Between President Xi's announcement of the BRI in September 2013 and June 30, 2016, Chinese state-owned enterprises—such as China Railway Group Limited and China Communications Construction Company Limited—have signed construction contracts for 38 large demonstration projects involving transport infrastructure covering 26 countries, and focusing on key land routes, port cooperation, and improvements in existing infrastructure. China has also launched 15 new airport projects and 28 airport expansion projects in the Chinese provinces along the Belt and Road.

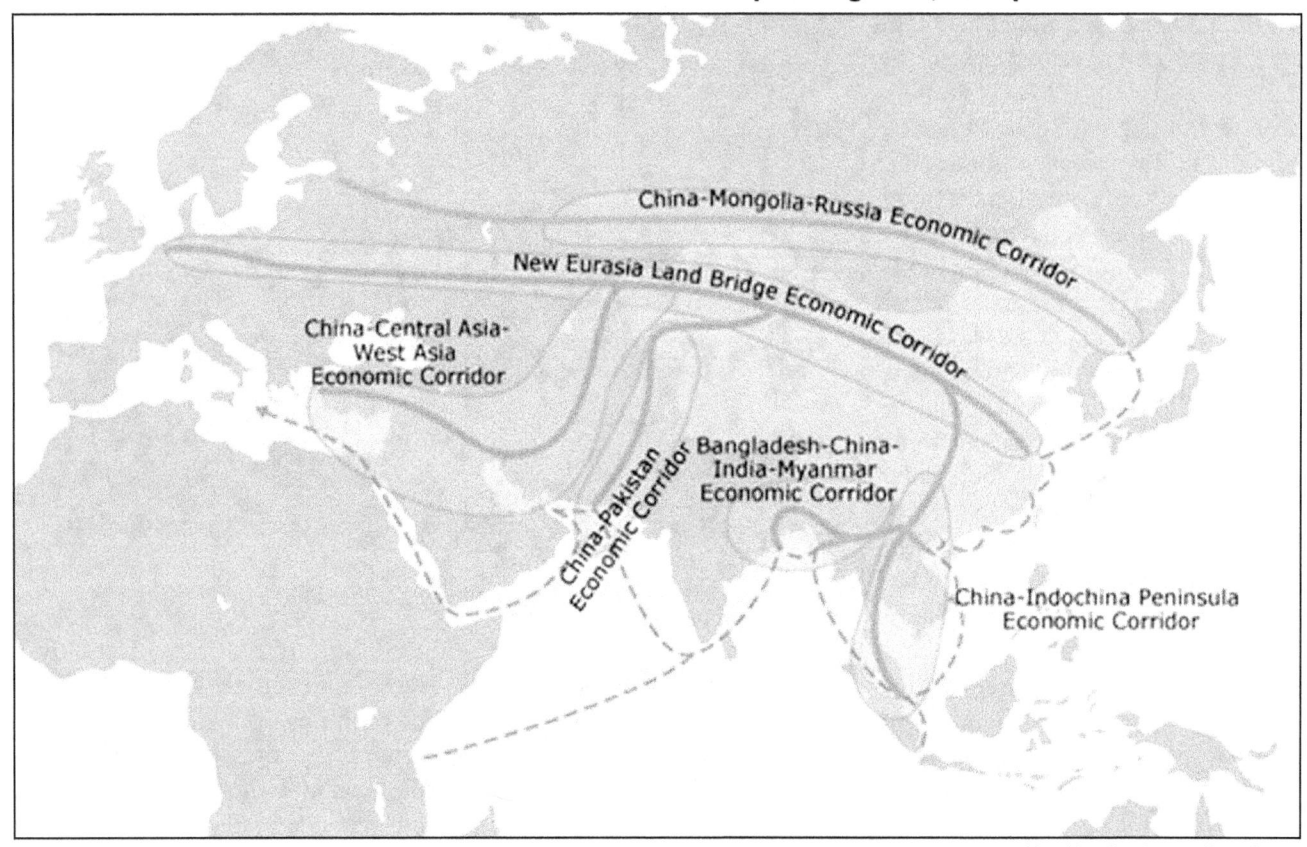

In addition to roads and rails, China is also providing much of the telecommunications along the routes. Telecom providers such as China Unicom, China Telecom, and China Mobile are speeding up cross-border transmission projects. In addition, the China-led TD-LTE networks for 4G mobile phones (also known as LTE-TDD) are operational in 30 countries, including China, the United States, Japan, India, Saudi Arabia, Russia, and Australia.

More Trade and Investment 'Along the Way'

The BRI has also greatly facilitated the increase of trade. From June 2013 to June 2016, China recorded $3.1 trillion in commodity trade along the Belt and Road, which accounts for 26 percent of China's total trade volume. As of June 2016, China had invested $51.1 billion total in these countries, accounting for 12% of Chinese overseas direct investment.

An important element in creating these development corridors is the establishment of industrial development zones and economic cooperation zones. As of June 30, 2016, five pilot zones for border opening-up and development have been established, in Dongxing near the border with Vietnam, Ruili near the Myanmar border, Erenhot on the border with Mongolia, Manzhouli on the Russian border, and the Port of Mongla, Bangladesh, on the Bay of Bengal.

Fifteen other *cross-border* economic cooperation areas are also now functioning in China—in Liaoning bordering North Korea (1), Jilin bordering North Korea and Russia (2), and Heilongjiang bordering Russia (2), all in northeast China; in Guangxi bordering Vietnam (2) and Yunnan also bordering Vietnam (4) in the south; and in Xinjiang on the Kazakstan border (4) in the northwest.

As of June of this year, China had reached agreement on 52 trade and economic cooperation zones within 18 countries along the routes of the Belt and Road, with a total investment of $16.5 billion. Among the thirteen zones that have been evaluated thus far, three are in full operation: the China-Belarus Industrial Park, the Thai-Chinese Rayong Industrial Zone, and the

Indonesia-China Integrated Industrial Parks. Other zones are in various stages of development in Cambodia, Vietnam, Pakistan, Zambia, Egypt, Nigeria, Ethiopia, and Hungary, as well as four planned zones in Russia. China has also signed cooperation agreements on "capacity sharing" in manufacturing with more than 20 countries along the Belt and Road.

Energy Projects

Over this initial three-year period, China has increased the pace of export of energy infrastructure to countries along the Belt and Road. From October 2013 to June 30, 2016, China's state-owned enterprises participated in the construction of 40 overseas energy projects, including power plants, electricity transmission facilities, and oil and gas pipelines, covering nineteen countries.

In 2014, construction of the Tajikistan part of the Central Asia-China Gas Pipeline and the Russian part of the Russia-China Gas Pipeline was set into motion. In 2015, Chinese nuclear power companies launched cooperation projects in Romania, Britain, Pakistan, and Argentina. Chinese hydropower companies also worked on projects in Angola, Brazil, Nepal, Pakistan, and Argentina. During the first half of 2016, China signed deals for 16 energy projects with countries along the Belt and Road.

Financing Development

The progress of the Silk Road Initiative has been greatly facilitated by the creation of new financial institutions devoted specifically to financing infrastructure investment. The Asian Infrastructure Investment Bank (AIIB), founded on December 2015, is the most important of these banks. With 57 member countries so far and an authorized capital of $100 billion, it has approved $509 million in investments in its first four projects, focusing on power, transportation, urban development, and other projects in Bangladesh, Indonesia, Pakistan, and Tajikistan.

The BRICS New Development Bank, established

Xinhua/Gao Bin

Technicians at work on the Ankara-Istanbul high-speed railway built by China Railway Construction Corporation, Jan. 6, 2014.

in July 2015 and headquartered in Shanghai, has an authorized capital of $100 billion and has already issued a first round of loans for so-called "clean energy" projects in China, India, Brazil, and South Africa.

The $40 billion Silk Road Fund had already been set up by the Chinese Government in December 2014 and has announced three sets of investments—to develop hydropower plants in Pakistan and other South Asian countries; to assist ChemChina, a Chinese chemical company, in acquiring Italian tire maker Pirelli; and to develop the Russia-based Yamal liquefied natural gas (LNG) project in the Russian Arctic region.

But the bulk of the funding for the Belt and Road is still being provided by the Chinese state development banks. China Development Bank has set up a Belt and Road project pool that encompasses more than 900 projects from over 60 countries in transportation, energy, resources, and other sectors. China's Export-Import Bank is financing more than 1,000 projects involving roads, railways, ports, power resources, pipelines, communications, and industrial parks in 49 of the countries along the Belt and Road. The China Export and Credit Insurance Corporation has supported export, domestic trade, and investment with a total value of $2.3 trillion, covering thousands of exporters and hundreds of medium- and long-term projects encompassing high technology export and large electro-machinery and equipment export.

Promoting the Development of Science

In addition to the industrial parks, the BRI is also intent on promoting the development of science in the countries along the routes. By June 2016, China had signed memoranda of understanding for scientific and technological cooperation in the areas of space, energy, and ecology with 56 Belt and Road countries. China has also established 38 science and technology centers in the form of smart industrial parks, joint laboratories, international technology transfer centers, and industrial cooperation and incubation centers.

The rapid development of the Chinese space program includes the construction of a space station, to be finished by 2022. It will also be open to the countries of the Belt and Road for the purpose of encouraging space exploration among those nations. Foreign astronauts will be invited to work on the Chinese space station, and several countries have already provided experiments for the Chinese Tiangong-2 space laboratory.

While the trans-Atlantic region still suffers from the turmoil of a bankrupt financial system, the Belt and Road Initiative is creating hope and optimism. What the developing sector failed to achieve during the four decades following the first calls for a New and Just Economic Order at the UN General Assembly in the 1970s, is now being accomplished, thanks to the success of one major developing country, China, which succeeded in working its way out of poverty and is now willing to share its secrets with the rest of the world.

Some people in the West have seen this as a threat. But, as Chinese leaders have been quick to point out, this is a win-win situation for everyone. If the Western nations—as some are beginning to do—view the BRI as an opportunity rather than a crisis, if they are prepared to break the stranglehold of the "too big to fail" banks over policy making and join in the project of rebuilding their collapsing infrastructure, they could transform the Silk Road project into a World Land-bridge. With this we could change the course of history and join with China in eliminating poverty from the human condition.

At Goa, BRICS Leaders Fight for Nuclear Power, and Against Destabilization

by Ramtanu Maitra

Oct. 23—The five BRICS heads of state assembled at Panjim, in India's State of Goa, on Oct 15-16 for deliberations on the ongoing and future plans of the BRICS member-nations on how to push ahead transportation and energy-related infrastructure, to build the foundation for an equitable development throughout the developing world, and thus to make the world secure. Their joint declaration, following this eighth such Summit, said: "We note the dynamic integration processes across the regions of the world, particularly in Asia, Africa and South America. We affirm our belief to promote growth in the context of regional integration on the basis of principles of equality, openness and inclusiveness. We further believe that this will promote economic expansion through enhanced trade and commercial and investment linkages.

PIB India

Leaders of the BRICS nations in Goa, India for the annual BRICS Summit, Oct. 16, 2016. In front (left to right) are Xi Jinping (China), Narendra Modi (India), and Vladimir Putin (Russia). Behind Putin are Jacob Zuma (South Africa) and Michel Temer (Brazil).

"We highlight the importance of public and private investments in infrastructure, including connectivity, to ensure sustained long-term growth. We, in this regard, call for approaches to bridge the financing gap in infrastructure, including through enhanced involvement of Multilateral Development Banks."

Summit at a Crucial Juncture

The Goa Summit was held at a time when the world has long been under the tutelage of the British empire, culminating in Obama's tyranny today. Abusing Roosevelt's 1944 Bretton Woods agreement that had promised development to the then-colonies, London and its satraps have brought the world to the verge of a total financial collapse, after refusing development in favor of almost a half-century of usurious looting. Faced with further pauperization and death, and badly needing the basic physical infrastructure to survive and grow, the five BRICS nations—Brazil, Russia, India, China and South Africa—representing almost 40 percent of world's population, have come together to concentrate their efforts to build the basic physical infrastructure of all developing nations.

The decades-long usurious looting of the develop-

Men flee as Qaddafi's tent burns behind them, Tripoli, Aug. 24, 2011.

Anti-government protesters at Maidan Square in Kiev, Ukraine, January 22, 2014.

ing nations by the British empire's powerful financial institutions, aided by the two major institutions set up by the Bretton Woods System, the International Monetary Fund (IMF) and the International Bank for Reconstruction and Development (IBRD, which later changed its name to become the World Bank), has not only perpetuated poverty, but has a created a sharply divided world, in which London's toadies are now threatening an all-annihilating nuclear war.

Destruction of Islamic Southwest Asia

Long before the BRIC grouping (South Africa joined in 2010) held its first formal summit in Yekaterinburg, Russia in 2009, the British-Saudi puppets Bush and Cheney had launched a full-fledged destructive war on Iraq in 2003. They created an environment that gave birth to a slew of terrorists, who later gelled together to form the Islamic State of Iraq and the Levant (ISIL) in 2013, and they sharpened the old sectarian divide among the Iraqis. Continuing the vicious policies to divide and destroy the Muslims of southwest Asia and North Africa, Obama (with fellow warrior-in-arms Hillary Clinton) launched another military assault, this time on Libya, in 2011. Another unprovoked military attack that not only destroyed a stable state, but also gave birth to a host of uncontrollable armed

terrorist groups exporting terrorism throughout southwest Asia and Africa. The Libyan terrorists and the other terrorists who emerged following the deliberate destruction of Iraq's economy and its security apparatus—and were financed by some of London's Gulf monarchies—have now succeeded in killing off hundreds of thousands in Syria, Iraq and Libya. Libya, which formerly had the highest per capita GDP and longest life expectancy on the continent—and fewer people below the poverty line than in the Netherlands—now has a population in despair and an economy in shambles. Thanks to that 2011 invasion which toppled and murdered the Libyan ruler Muammar Qaddafi, thousands of Libyans have become homeless and at least a million have left their country to settle in Egypt, Tunisia and elsewhere.

Target: Russia

In 2011, to complete the destruction of southwest Asia, Britain, France and Obama's United States engaged themselves in yet another project. Its objective was to remove the Bashar al-Assad-led Syrian regime through covert operations, using terrorists brought in from Libya and Iraq, and delivered by Saudi Arabia and Qatar. After beginning by feeding bloodthirsty terrorists who are in league with the degenerate British-Saudi monarchies, Obama and puppets have since remained engaged in a war that has already killed almost half a million people by some accounts, and has turned large parts of Syria into rubble. These five years of ongoing destruction of southwest Asia, were a project masterminded by the British Throne, and carried out by Obama's United States, Britain and France.

Long before the BRICS came into existence, the City of London and its minions had engaged in another destructive policy, targeting Russia. This project involved undermining and threatening Russia by expanding London's military arm, NATO, throughout Eastern Europe, so as to militarily encircle Russia. With this objective in mind, the EU and Bush-Cheney's United States had orchestrated the 2004 Orange Revolution in Ukraine. In addition to Ukraine, the 2003 Rose Revolution in Georgia and the 2005 Tulip Revolution in Kyrgyzstan, also had Washington's paw-prints all over them. Such unsettling geopolitical moves by Washington on Russia's doorsteps, have led some Russian analysts to believe that Obama is indeed seeking regime-change in Moscow itself. He is.

John J. Mearsheimer, in his essay, "Why the Ukraine Crisis is the West's Fault," in the Sept.-Oct. 2014 issue of *Foreign Affairs*, had noted that since the mid-1990s, Russian leaders have adamantly opposed NATO enlargement, and in recent years, they have made it clear that they would not stand by while their strategically important neighbor Ukraine was turned into a Washington bastion. For Putin, the illegal overthrow of Ukraine's democratically elected president —which he rightly labeled a "coup"—was the final straw. He responded by taking back Crimea, a peninsula he feared would host a NATO naval base. Throwing caution to the winds and hell-bent to confront Russia, the Obama administration, with the tacit approval of the EU, has now brought the Ukraine crisis they created, to the very brink of a nuclear war with Russia.

But the Russian involvement in Syria in support of its internationally recognized government, is thwarting the British-French-U.S.-led effort to usher in anarchy and further the proliferation of terrorism throughout the region, through regime-change in Damascus. Obama is also deeply concerned about Russia's growing relations with China, a power to reckon with, and Russia's important role in the BRICS. Between Russia, China and India, the three most powerful nations in Eurasia, a vast swath of land is now slipping out of geopolitical control of the British Empire.

The BRICS Provides Optimism

It is in this complex environment that the BRICS has begun to grow. While the overhanging threat of war is making this world an increasingly dangerous place, still, the BRICS member nations have put together a program to infuse optimism among those whose hopes and dreams have been shattered by these brutal policies, which have used the broken-down Bretton Woods System and indiscriminate military actions to achieve their end. The BRICS leaders have determined that a world dominated by economically weak trans-Atlantic powers, which are ready to go to any extent to undermine others' efforts to grow, requires security. In order to ensure security, particularly in Eurasia, the BRICS has joined hands with the Shanghai Cooperation Organization (SCO), an organization formed in 2001 by China, Russia, and five "stan" nations of Central Asia. Recently, two major South Asian nations, India and Pakistan, have been inducted as full members in the SCO. The stated mission of the SCO is to ensure security in Eurasia through cultural and social interactions.

Beyond accessing the reach that the SCO provides, the BRICS member-nations have included various partners, including non-BRICS countries and their associations, to extend their reach to smaller regional nations. The initial outreach effort took place in 2013 at the Durban summit in South Africa, with the invitation to leaders from African states, to the African Union, and to sub-regional associations of African nations. In 2014, Fortaleza, Brazil, was the venue for a dialogue between the leaders of the BRICS and twelve South and Central American countries. At the BRICS' Ufa Summit in Russia in 2015, all the leaders of the SCO, both members and observers, as well as the members of the Eurasian Economic Union (Belarus, Kazakstan, Armenia, Kyrgyzstan, and Russia), plus Azerbaijan and Turkmenistan, were present to meet with the five BRICS leaders.

In 2016 in Panjim, Goa, the host nation, India, had invited the member-nations of the Bay of Bengal Initiative for Multi-Sectoral Technical and Economic Cooperation (BIMSTEC), including Bangladesh, Myanmar, Sri Lanka, Thailand, Bhutan and Nepal besides India,

IAEA/Petr Pavlicek

The 500 megawatt fast breeder nuclear reactor at the Kalpakkam Nuclear Complex in Tamil Nadu, southern India, now just months away from operation.

to interact with the BRICS leaders. BIMSTEC, as its name suggests, is an economic grouping, and it encompasses not only South Asian nations but also two Southeast Asian countries.

At the Fortaleza Summit in 2014, a ground breaking event in the short history of the BRICS, member nations set about to loosen the deadly stranglehold that the IMF/World Bank has imposed on the developing countries. It is not an easy task, but the BRICS took up the challenge. At Fortaleza, the participating heads of state created the New Development Bank (NDB, also known as the BRICS Bank) to finance the weak physical infrastructure of most of Asia, Africa and Ibero-America. The task is challenging, since various reports indicate that in Asia alone an investment to the tune of $9 trillion is necessary to ensure future economic development. A recently released Citi GPS report, entitled "Infrastructure for Growth: The Dawn of a New Multi-Trillion Dollar Asset Class," estimates a global need for infrastructure spending of $59 trillion over the next 15 years.

BRICS Bank and CRA

The NDB's initial authorized capital is $100 billion, divided into one million shares having a par value of $100,000 each. The initial subscribed capital of the NDB is $50 billion, divided into paid-in shares (of $10 billion), and the initial subscribed capital of the bank was equally distributed among the founding members.

At Fortaleza, the BRICS leaders also created a Contingent Reserve Arrangement (CRA) for the provision of support through liquidity and precautionary instruments, in response to actual or potential short-term balance of payments pressures—i.e. currency warfare as by George Soros in 1997-98 for example. Initially, it was decided that CRA will have total committed resources of $100 billion. In his address to the BRICS Finance Ministers in Washington on Oct. 7, India's Finance Minister Arun Jaitley said that the BRICS' CRA is now operational to deal with any short-term balance of payments pressures the grouping's member nations may face.

Although the NDB is still in a fledgling state, the good news is that months before the Goa Summit—that is less than two years after it was created at Fortaleza—the Bank had already approved its first loans of $811 million for "renewable energy" projects in Brazil, China, India and South Africa, Russian news agencies reported last April. In addition, the NDB President told Reuters on the fringes of the 2016 BRICS Summit that the Bank is ready to lend $ 2-2.5 billion in 2017. Compare this with the IBRD's (World Bank's) lending history in the 1940s. After it was established in 1944, the IBRD's first loans were extended during the late 1940s to finance the reconstruction of the war-ravaged economies of Western Europe. While the IBRD kept its development funding within Western Europe, the NDB's loans have already included three Continents.

BRICS for Nuclear Power

In addition to its objective of developing a growth-oriented bank, the NDB—which saves countries from the "IMF conditionalities" which force them to abandon all essential capital-intensive development projects—the BRICS member-nations have also emphasized the necessity to enhance capital-intensive nuclear energy for clean and safe power generation. Over the recent decades, the trans-Atlantic nations, which were the pioneers of nuclear power generation, have been guided by anti-development leaders, and have allowed themselves to be confused to the point of being controlled by the Greenies. As a result, they have abandoned the building of nuclear power reactors, and have opted to rely increasingly on high-priced, inefficient and intermittent so-called "renewable" power sources. This has now reached the point, that even if at some future time these nations were once again to seek nuclear power for their basic survival, they will have to import nuclear reactors! By contrast, the BRICS nations have begun to move confidently towards embracing nuclear power, with its low running cost and high efficiency, for their future economic development.

The need for nuclear power was also reflected in the Goa Declaration, which included the following paragraph: "We recognize that nuclear energy will play a significant role for some of the BRICS countries in meeting their 2015 Paris Climate Change Agreement commitments, and for reducing global greenhouse gas emissions in the long term. In this regard, we underline the importance of predictability in accessing technology and finance for expansion of civil nuclear energy capacity which would contribute to the sustainable development of BRICS countries."

For BRICS member-nations, commitment to nuclear energy for power generation is not just rhetoric. China is committed now more than ever to make nuclear power its main source of electrical power in the years to come. According to *World Nuclear News* ("Nuclear Power in the World Today: August 2016"), the Chinese government plans to increase nuclear generating capacity to 58 GWe, with 30 GWe more under construction by 2021. "China has completed construction and commenced operation of over 30 new nuclear power reactors since 2002, and some 20 new reactors are under construction. These include the world's first four Westinghouse AP1000 units, and a demonstration high-temperature gas-cooled reactor plant. Many more are planned, with construction due to start within about three years. China is commencing export marketing of a largely indigenous reactor design. R&D on nuclear reactor technology in China is second to none."

India is another country now moving steadfastly to utilize its indigenous and imported reactors to make nuclear energy an important element of its electrical power sector. According to the Modi Government's projection, India, now with 6 GWe installed nuclear power capacity, is planning to move quickly to install 63 GWe by 2030. Its short-term target is to put 14.5 Gwe of nuclear capacities on line by 2020. "These reactors include light- and heavy-water reactors as well as fast reactors. In addition to the 22 online, of both indigenous and foreign design, five power reactors are under construction, including a 500 MWe prototype fast-breeder reactor. This will take India's ambitious thorium program to stage two, and set the scene for eventual utilization of the country's abundant thorium to fuel reactors," *World Nuclear News* reported. India is now in the process of finalizing about 30 GWe of imported reactors to be installed. These reactors will be provided by Russia, Westinghouse, GE, and Areva (of France), if and when negotiations come to successful completion. Moreover, India is actively seeking both Japan's and China's cooperation in this sector.

Another major nation within the BRICS, Russia, is steadily increasing its nuclear capacity and, according to *World Nuclear News*, plans to have an installed capacity of 30.5 GWe. In addition, Russia, having long been at the forefront of advanced nuclear technology, is now the world leader in reactor exports, building and financing nuclear power plants around the globe. Russia's nuclear-power diplomacy has become very important. Countries that have signed on to Rosatom nuclear agreements span all regions of the world, and include strategically significant nations such as Argentina, Iran, Egypt, Saudi Arabia, Vietnam, Bangladesh, Jordan and Turkey, among others. As of 2014, 29 Russian reactors are planned for construction abroad, and Rosatom predicts that the number will grow to around 80 within a few years.

In essence, at the eighth BRICS Summit at Goa, the BRICS leaders rallied to ensure that the dying London-centered empire of Obama, is replaced by a world governed by equality and mutual respect for the interests of large and small states in both West and East, mutual economic gains, cultural compatibility and reciprocal enrichment of civilizations.

II. The Law of Hamilton and LaRouche Is Natural Law

The LaRouche-Hamilton Laws Will Solve Today's Crisis

by Robert Ingraham

Oct. 23—On October 7, 2016, in a discussion with associates, and following several reports on the unfolding breakdown of the trans-Atlantic banking and financial system, Lyndon LaRouche stated the following,

> All you have to do is to take my laws, which I presented. Those laws, my laws, define exactly what solves the problem by creating a standard by which credit is defined. This was developed by the Treasurer of the United States [Alexander Hamilton]. This is the only way it will work...

> All you have to do is go for an international program based on that principle, the same principle, and you've got to get the people of the nations working together to understand what this kind of action is. Just read the publications on law by [Hamilton]. He wrote the laws. They're written there. But people don't do it. They talk about something else. Therefore, they don't understand what makes history, what makes history work. What I did was actually a mechanism to define the way in which the original system had been established. By Hamilton. You don't have to do anything else. That's what you have to do...

> You're talking about Hamilton's laws, and you're talking about my laws. That's what you're talking about. Don't change the subject...

> You have to get an international agreement among nations, among a significant number of

Lyndon H. LaRouche, Jr.

> nations, which will create a credit system, an international credit system or something tantamount to that, which will deal with this problem. We're not talking about that, yet. You have to talk about that; you've got to talk about the work of Hamilton. You've got to put the name of Hamilton in there, and you've got to put my name in there.

> Because that's the only way you're going to get that thing done.

> Get some books about Hamilton's economy. It's all there. All I did was to put this thing into standards which conform to what Hamilton laid out. People have to take the handbooks, the records of Hamilton; read those things as Hamilton stipulates. Use that. Do it! Then you can go to the table and say, "Now we can create a credit system." Take Hamilton, and take what I have done. Put the two things together, and that work contains enough information to define exactly what has to be done. It's just ignored because people want to be stupid.

Let us be as clear as possible on the most crucial point. What is being discussed here, what Mr. LaRouche is proposing, is not "economic theory." It is an *Action Plan*, a solution to the current trans-Atlantic financial and banking crisis. It will work, but it will work only if the precise method prescribed by Mr. LaRouche is followed. It is, in fact, the only way out of our current crisis.

I. Hamilton's Reports and LaRouche's Four Laws

Between January of 1790 and December of 1791, that is, over a period of a mere twenty-four months, Alexander Hamilton authored five documents which created the sovereign United States of America and brought into existence a national Public Credit System, entirely new in the history of the human species.

These documents are:

- January 14, 1790—the *Report on Public Credit*
- December 14, 1790—the *Second Report on Public Credit* (the Report on a National Bank)
- January 28, 1791—the *Report on the Establishment of a Mint*
- February 23, 1791—an *Opinion as to the Constitutionality of the Bank of the United States*
- December 5, 1791—the *Report on Manufactures*.

Much more will be said about these documents later in this article, but for now only a few observations need be made.

George Washington was inaugurated as the first President of the United States on April 30, 1789. At that time, the new government, as established by the recently ratified U.S. Constitution, was not even functioning. The nation was *de facto* bankrupt, its currency debased and its finances in a state of chaos. This was the crisis that Alexander Hamilton, as the new Secretary of Treasury, was tasked to solve. Hamilton's measures and his actions were entirely successful. What is more, however, is that Hamilton did not simply implement means to solve a "financial crisis"; he brought into existence—created—a system of Public Credit whereby a sweeping future-oriented transformation of both the nation's physical economy *as well as the culture of the nation* might be accomplished.

On June 8, 2014, the LaRouche Political Action Committee published a document, authored by Lyndon LaRouche, titled, "The Four New Laws to Save the

Alexander Hamilton

U.S.A. Now! Not an Option: an Immediate Necessity." In that policy statement, LaRouche begins by saying, *"The economy of the United States of America, and also that of the trans-Atlantic political-economic regions of the planet are now under the immediate mortal danger of a general, physical- economic, chain-reaction breakdown crisis of that region of this planet as a whole."*

Mr. LaRouche goes on to describe the nature and the origins for this physical-economic as well as financial/banking crisis, and then he proceeds to enunciate what he terms "The Available Remedies." In lieu of reprinting that entire document here, we present just the briefest synopsis of what LaRouche proposes:

- The immediate re-enactment of the Glass-Steagall law instituted by President Franklin D. Roosevelt, without modification, as to principle of action;
- A return to a system of top-down, and thoroughly defined [as] National Banking;
- The purpose of the use of a Federal Credit-system is to generate high-productivity trends in improvements of employment, with the accompanying intention, to increase the physical-economic productivity, and the standard of living of persons and households of the United States; and
- Adopt a Fusion-Driver "Crash Program," later defined to include the relaunching of the space program. "The essential distinction of man from all lower forms of life, hence, in practice, is that it presents the means for the perfection of the specifically affirmative aims and needs of human individual and social life...."

If the reader of this article will take the time to read the full document published by Lyndon LaRouche in 2014, and then proceed to read and study the reports issued by Alexander Hamilton in 1790 and 1791, the full coherence of what LaRouche and Hamilton are proposing will become very clear, particularly as to matters of principle.

II. Historical Specificity

It is strongly recommended to read the five documents authored by Hamilton that are listed at the beginning of this report in *chronological* order. The benefit in doing so is to experience how Hamilton proceeds step-by-step in the creation of his system. True, some of what he discusses is specific to the time and circumstances within which he lived—such as in his discussion of gold and silver coins in the *Report on the Mint*—but that is the point. Hamilton is not writing timeless academic economic theory. He is dealing with a crisis, and he is defining the way, the only lawful and effective way, to overcome that crisis.

To truly understand what Hamilton is doing, one must look out through *his* eyes. In many of his writings from 1790 through 1794, Hamilton is very explicit that Jefferson and his allies are intent on overturning the 1788 Constitution. Everything they did was directed toward that end. Thus, Hamilton's banking and economic writings of 1790-1792 are not ivory tower speculations. They are written under war-time conditions.

The Battlefield

In early 1791, Thomas Jefferson released his *Opinion on the Constitutionality of a National Bank*. This was not a mere critique of Hamilton's proposal for a National Bank. It was the opening salvo of all out war to defeat Hamilton, destroy the Washington Administration and overturn the Constitution that had been ratified only two years earlier. Jefferson's declaration of war against Hamilton would unleash what became an open rebellion against the Washington Administration, including an armed insurrection against the U.S. Government—known euphemistically as the "Whiskey Rebellion"—and widespread anti-Washington and anti-Hamilton riots in 1794-1795. This would culminate in the assassination of Hamilton in 1804.

It is sometimes stated by illiterate historians that, "Hamilton was for manufacturing, and Jefferson was for agriculture." What a lie! Hamilton was for human progress, human advancement, science and industry; Jefferson was for slavery and enforced human backwardness. It is also useful to note that the greatest enemy of Hamilton's *demand* for scientific and manufacturing progress are the proposals put forth by the British Empire's Adam Smith in his *Wealth of Nations*. Everything Smith proposes, on behalf of his British

masters, is contrary to the approach which Hamilton initiated.

Every step of the way, beginning with the proposal of Madison's pro-slavery anti-national "Virginia Plan" at the Constitutional Convention in 1788, through Hamilton's proposal for the National Government to assume the debt of the individual states and unify the finances of the nation, through his defense of "government corporations," and into his proposal for "bounties" in the *Report on Manufactures*, Hamilton was at war with those who favored sectionalism, slavery, a weak national government and unchecked financial speculation. His adversaries included the British Empire, the southern slavocracy and the corrupt swindlers of what later became known as Wall Street—the friends of Aaron Burr.

It was under these—the most adverse — conditions that Hamilton set about, beginning in 1790, to erect his new system.

III. Hamilton's Laws

As one makes one's way through Hamilton's five documents, the effect is of entering into the mind of a great architect, as Hamilton sets out to create the nation. Each tier creates the basis for the next tier, with the vision of the completed edifice always in mind from the start. The end intention determines all of the preliminary and subsequent steps.

He begins at the beginning. The nation is bankrupt. In the *Report on Public Credit* he provides the evidence of this bankruptcy, he defines the moral and legal issues at stake, and he defines the solution as one of securing a well- funded and secure public debt, one which will meet all obligations. He articulates a detailed plan of tariffs, taxation and other measures to ensure that all *bona fide* debt obligations will be met and confidence in the nation's credit restored. He states that this is the pre-condition for a desired revival of trade and promotion of agriculture and manufacturing.

During the Revolution, the Continental Congress had borrowed heavily from the French government and from Dutch bankers, but the government, from a lack of revenue, had stopped paying both principal and interest on those debts in 1786. By 1789, the nation's foreign debt totaled $12 million dollars, and its domestic debt—a combination of state debt, bills of credit, and various notes and certificates—stood at $65 million.

Even worse, the new government lacked the funds to operate day-to-day.

Between September and December of 1789, Hamilton secured loans, totaling $170,000, from the Bank of New York and the Bank of North America,[1] to cover the salaries of the President, the Vice-President, Congress and other necessary functions. Then, in January of 1790, he issued his *Report on Public Credit*.

Sovereign Debt

Hamilton's aim, in this Report, is threefold. The first is to stop the hemorrhaging, to prevent the nation from descending into financial and economic chaos. The second is to unify the finances of the nation, to eradicate all sectional and local authority over matters of public credit. The third goal, one which Hamilton will proceed to address more directly in the *Second Report on Public Credit* (the Report on a National Bank), is to create the basis for an expanding system of public credit *generation*, for the purpose of developing the physical economic potentials of the nation.

Hamilton is ironclad in his demand that all government debts—state, local, national and foreign—will be paid at full value. The details of his proposal are multifaceted and comprehensive, and it is not possible to fully elaborate on them here. He proposes a series of very detailed steps, all of which are designed to provide confidence in the nation's credit, as well as to generate low-interest capital for investment in the nation's economy.

It is in this Report that Hamilton also establishes the basic principle that the nation's public debt, if properly funded, will provide the basis for the generation of new

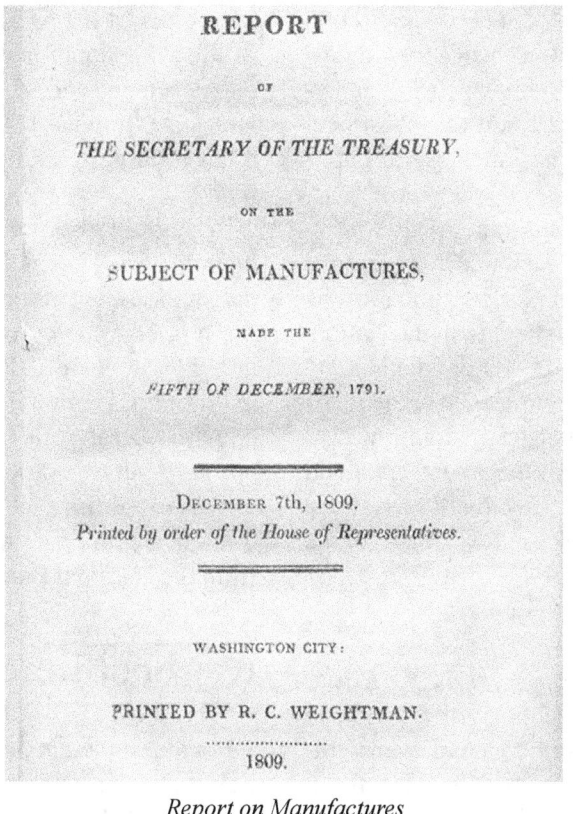

REPORT

OF

THE SECRETARY OF THE TREASURY,

ON THE

SUBJECT OF MANUFACTURES,

MADE THE

FIFTH OF DECEMBER, 1791.

DECEMBER 7th, 1809.
Printed by order of the House of Representatives.

WASHINGTON CITY:

PRINTED BY R. C. WEIGHTMAN.

1809.

Report on Manufactures

credit that will stimulate investment and economic development.

A key component of Hamilton's plan—one fiercely opposed by Jefferson, Madison and Monroe—was for the National government to assume the millions of dollars in individual state debts. This would have the effect of transforming all of the state debt holders into national debt holders, solidifying the position and sovereignty of the National government. This was accomplished with the United States Funding Act of 1790, through which $21 million of state debt was taken over by the National government. Under this act, the states were given extremely generous terms, and the shedding of their debt burden left the states with substantial revenue, earned through the federal securities, enabling them to directly invest in industry and promote economic enterprises.

National Credit

In his *Report on a National Bank*, Hamilton next proceeds to the issue of Sovereign credit generation as the essential life-spring for the new republic. There is no substitute for reading this report, and a mere commentary does it an injustice. Suffice it to say that Hamilton makes short shrift of all the objections to the Bank, defines the principles upon which it will operate, and then he proceeds to enunciate a twenty-four point detailed plan for the actual day-to-day operations of the bank.

It is toward the end of the *Report* that Hamilton first introduces his proposal to use the funded debt of the nation—a funded debt which he, himself, had established with the *First Report on Public Credit* and the Funding Act of 1790—as the means to provide new credit for manufacturing, agriculture, trade and other useful enterprises, thus establishing a *National Public Credit System*.

Under Hamilton's proposal, a percentage of the sov-

---

1. The Bank of New York was founded by Hamilton, and the Bank of North America was founded by Hamilton's ally Robert Morris.

ereign debt of the United States (up to $2 million) will be deposited as assets in the new Bank. These funds will then allow the Bank to issue notes, as loans, for the financing of many useful enterprises. The notes could also be deposited with other financial institutions as well as circulate among businesses, establishing a sound financial market and integrating the entire financial system of the nation into a nationally directed Public Credit System. Security of the notes would be guaranteed, since their issuance was based entirely on the sovereign debt obligations of the National government.

It should be noted, that in both the *First* and *Second Reports on Public Credit*, Hamilton spends a good deal of time on the need to create a system which will generate large amounts of *low-interest* credit for investment in manufacturing, agriculture and other useful enterprises.

The immediate effect of Hamilton's plan was to create a legal, sound banking system, under continuous national review, with the intention for providing for the rapid physical-economic development of the nation. Hamilton is keenly aware of the power of banking and the power of credit to foster economic development. At the same time, as proven by his later writings and actions, Hamilton is explicit that all illegal, unsound and shady financial practices will be choked off through the deployment of the National Bank as the regulator of the nation's credit system.

Nation-Building

Hamilton's third Report, the *Report on the Establishment of a Mint*, is of too technical of a nature to elaborate here, but it should not be passed over without comment. In these first three *Reports*, Hamilton moves from securing the credit of the nation, to national banking, and then to the currency itself. There is a progression, a lawful creation of a national system of banking and credit. Hamilton is extraordinarily precise as he moves, step-by-step, in erecting his system. Nothing is arbitrary. All of the actions are of one design.

Then, in December of 1791 came the *Report on Manufactures*. It is here that the completed nature of Hamilton's *Public Credit* system comes to light. This *Report* contains the famous "Section VIII: The Encouragement of New Inventions and Discoveries," where Hamilton defines the Constitutional responsibility of the government to transform the nation—as a matter of permanent ongoing willful policy—to promote the scientific and industrial development of the nation. Hamilton is very explicit as to the genuine power and mission of the National government to promote these changes. There are many passages in the *Report* which make all of this very clear, but rather than cite lengthy quotations here, it were better left to the reader to obtain a copy of the *Report* and investigate the matter for one's self.

To achieve his end, Hamilton takes an additional step beyond his proposals in the *Report on a National Bank*. He proposes to supplement the credit generating power of the National Bank by using two percent of the funded national debt, every year, directly to finance science and industry, in the form of "bounties." He asks, "In what can the national debt be so useful, as in prompting and improving the efforts of industry?"

Hamilton also proposes the creation of a "national manufactory," i.e., not simply the financing of individual factories, but the creation of a centralized hub where the most advanced forms of technology and industry might be developed. Simultaneous with the writing of this Report, Hamilton initiated the founding of the *Society for Establishing Useful Manufactures*, as an attempt to put this proposal into motion, and he led the effort to establish a pilot project at Paterson, New Jersey through a combination of private investment and loans from the National Bank.

IV. Constitutional Lawfulness

In the above-cited October 7 quotation from Lyndon LaRouche, he states, "All you have to do is to take my laws, which I presented. Those laws, my laws, define exactly what solves the problem by creating a standard by which credit is defined. This was developed by the Treasurer of the United States [Alexander Hamilton]. This is the only way it will work... Just read the publications on law by Hamilton. He wrote the laws."

LaRouche's use of the term "laws," as opposed to "policy" or "program," or some other similar term, may seem odd or eccentric to the lazy reader, but it is not LaRouche who originates this concept of lawfulness; it is precisely the approach insisted upon by Hamilton, himself. This is nowhere more clear than in his *Opinion as to the Constitutionality of the Bank of the United States*.

There are, in fact, two parallel and intertwined concepts of lawfulness to consider here. One is Hamilton's insistence that not only are all of his measures lawful, but that the contrary proposals of Jefferson, *et al.*, are unlawful because they are contrary to the species-nature of the Republic that was created at the Constitutional Convention in 1788. The very nature of the sovereign Republic which came into existence in 1789 demands the Public Credit System that Hamilton defines in his *Reports*. The contrary proposals put forth by Jefferson and Madison are more in tune with what would later emerge as the Confederate States of America in 1861.

Public domain/Davidt8

First Bank of the United States (1797-1811), 120 South Third Street, Philadelphia, Pennsylvania.

The second thing to recognize is that Hamilton's policies are lawful simply because they work. And they represent the only approach that will work. They worked then, and Lyndon LaRouche's redefining of Hamilton's Laws will work today.

Hamilton's Argument

One thing that leaps off the page in reading his *Reports* is that Hamilton continually makes the point, not only of the necessity for his initiatives, but of the Constitutional legality of everything he is proposing. For the perceptive reader, what becomes clear is that Hamilton is not proposing individual pieces of legislation, nor simply particular banking measures—he is defining the actual Constitutional Nature of the Republic. His argument is that legality is to be found in the actual dynamic *intent* of the Constitution itself. It is very instructive to witness Hamilton's lawful—as Einstein would understand the term *lawful*—and relentless pursuit of his goal.

No arbitrary actions are allowed. No tyrannical actions. Every action, beginning with the assumption of Revolutionary War and State debts, through to the pro-

posals within the *Report on Manufactures*, follows a lawful progression. It is a mandatory path that must be followed.

Following the release of Hamilton's *Report on a National Bank*, that document came under violent attack from Thomas Jefferson, James Madison and other apologists for the southern slavocracy. The focus of these attacks was their denial of the right of the National Government to establish, by law, corporations, since there was no specific "enumerated" right named in the Constitution granting the government that specific right.

Hamilton's argument, one earlier enunciated by Gouverneur Morris, is that the *General Welfare Clause*, within the body of the U.S. Constitution, provides all of the legal backing required for the government to take *any lawful action*—not arbitrary, but lawful—in pursuit of the intentions of that Constitution, as adopted at Philadelphia in 1788.

In his *Opinion*, Hamilton states,

Every power vested in a government is in its nature sovereign, and includes, by force of the term, a right to employ all the means requisite and fairly applicable to the attainment of the ends of such power, and which are not precluded by restrictions and exceptions specified in the Constitution, or not immoral, or not contrary to the essential ends of political society.

And, in his *Vindication of the Funding System*, written later in the summer of 1792, Hamilton goes even further, stating,

[All property rights] which are contrary to the social order, and to the permanent welfare of society ought to be abolished...

Whenever, indeed, a right of property is infringed for the general good, if the nature of the case admits of compensation, it ought to be made; but if compensation be impracticable, that impracticability ought not to be an obstacle to a clearly essential reform.

This does not imply that the government may do anything it chooses, as in the call by Jefferson and others to repudiate Revolutionary War debt. It means that the sovereign power of the National government can and must be employed on behalf of the intent of the Constitution, which, itself, is coherent with Natural Law. Within that intent, as Hamilton defines in his *Opinion as to the Constitutionality of the Bank of the United States*, the power of the National government is awesome.

V. The LaRouche-Hamilton Solution

As LaRouche states, "My laws, define exactly what solves the problem by creating a standard by which credit is defined." To reiterate, in the briefest sketch-synopsis, those Laws are: Glass-Steagall, National Banking, a Federal Credit system to generate high-productivity trends in improvements of employment, and a Fusion-Driver and space "Crash Program." This is the Hamiltonian solution to today's crisis. It worked in 1790-1792. It will work today.

The axiomatic flaw of almost all modern financiers and economists is that they do not assign a true "human value" to any financial investment. Their system is valueless and mathematical. Thus, misguided fools would define the problem we face today as "How to fix the banking system." That approach can lead into all kinds of hare-brained schemes, many of which would leave intact the oligarchical system of usury and speculation.

That is not Hamilton's approach. That is not LaRouche's approach.

Consider the question of reimposing Glass-Steagall and so-called "banking reform." As Lyndon LaRouche has forcefully insisted, Glass-Steagall is a vital necessary step, a precondition, for a return to both sound—Constitutional—banking practices, as well as a genuine economic recovery. But it is not "banking reform" legislation! It represents a Constitutional Principle, one indispensable for the future development of the population.

On the other hand, defining Glass-Steagall as synonymous with a simple "banking reform" is sophistry. Yes, under Glass-Steagall, we will separate out the viable elements of the *commercial* banking system. We will regulate them, reform them, and integrate them into a viable National Credit System, much as President Franklin Roosevelt did in 1933. We will then create a system of National Banking and Public Credit, as Hamilton did.

But do the investment banks, the hedge funds, and the other gambling houses serve any necessary *lawful* purpose, as such lawfulness is defined by Hamilton? Or, better, might they not be shuttered, "with or without compensation" for their gambling debts? Recall, first, that "investment banking" is the descendent of the centuries-old British system of merchant banking, a system completely alien and hostile to Hamilton's conception of National Banking. Recall, also, that virtually all of the current financial practices of these institutions—derivatives, options trading, financial speculation—were illegal under President Roosevelt. One must ask one's self, "What is the underlying Law which must govern the affairs of the nation, or a community of nations?"

Future Generations

Hamilton's rigorous approach, in his *Reports*, of identifying *legitimate* debt, sound banking, Constitutional credit generation, and scientific and industrial progress has stood the test of time. It is future orientated. What is being built? What is being created? What is being transformed? This must be the necessary orientation.

As Lyndon LaRouche states, in his *Four Laws*:

The purpose of the use of a Federal Credit-system, is to generate high-productivity trends in improvements of employment, with the accompanying intention, to increase the physical-economic productivity, and the standard of living of persons and households of the United States.

Today, tens of millions of Americans are standing at a precipice, overlooking an abyss, as living standards, health care, education, and the nation's culture vanish. Heroin and other drugs are everywhere. These same Americans know that the worst is still to come. Hopelessness and fear are spreading throughout American society. The nation of China, on the other hand, has elevated 800 million of her people out of poverty during just the last 20 to 30 years, and is now leading the world in science, space exploration and economic development.

This destruction of the population in the trans-Atlantic world must be reversed. The entire population must be uplifted, in terms of its standard of living, its access to "high productivity" employment, but also in its access to classical education and its exposure to those creative inputs in science and in the arts which will provoke creative investigations and breakthroughs within the individual human mind.

On May 10, 2016, during a discussion with supporters in Manhattan, Lyndon LaRouche addressed this precise issue, stating,

It comes in the ability of mankind, to develop within the human individual the characteristics to give a higher degree of power to mankind as a whole, through self-development of the human species. That's the only thing that is important . . .

The issue is, can the human species produce from within its own ranks a body of people who will meet the challenge of defeating the kind of evil we have to face now . . .

Mankind is not a bunch of objects that you can manipulate and make the toys dance for you. That does not work. You actually have to create a power in mankind which is improved over previously existing expressions of mankind. That is the whole game. And you have to

spread this kind of development, such that it sustains itself.

Hamilton's creation of a system of Constitutional Public Credit solved the financial/economic crisis of his day, but it is also important to recognize that in so doing, he defined the advancement of the population—that is, the ongoing cognitive development of the population—as the axiomatic law of the new Republic. This is explicit in both the *Opinion as to the Constitutionality of the Bank of the United States* and the *Report on Manufactures*. The uplifting of the population, the enhancement of their potentials, in a permanent, ongoing way, is the true Hamiltonian nature of the American Republic. It is, in fact, the *Law of the Republic*, and anything opposed to that is illegal and unconstitutional.

That is what must be done. Any other approach is un-lawful and un-Constitutional. Hamilton defined the Laws by which the economy and the banking system must function. Lyndon LaRouche's Twenty-First Century redefinition of Hamilton's approach, in his *Four Laws*, shows the way into the future.

III. Obama Has Totally Failed

Duterte Crushes the Obama/Hillary Imperial Pivot to Asia

by Michael Billington

Oct. 24 (EIRNS)—The newly elected President of the Philippines, Rodrigo Duterte, in a press conference at the beginning of his visit to China on Oct. 18, described the reasoning behind the transformation of his country's foreign policy from subservience to U.S. dictates to alignment with China's New Silk Road concept of win-win development of the world as a whole. (A transcript of portions of Duterte's remarks is included below.) At the same time, he presented a powerful indictment of Obama, Bush, Tony Blair, and the British Empire for crimes against humanity—an unprecedented and courageous act for a head of state. The truth of his indictment was clearly contained in the indictment itself.

Obama's plan for war against Russia and China has been dealt a powerful blow by Duterte's courage. The threat began with Obama's "Pivot to Asia," announced by then Secretary of State Hillary Clinton in 2011, a plan to militarily encircle China with U.S. nuclear forces, together with an economic isolation of China (the Trans-Pacific Partnership, TPP). The centerpiece of the policy was to be the transformation of the Philippines into a vast U.S. military base, an "unsinkable aircraft carrier."

The Philipines was then governed by a puppet of Obama's Wall Street and British controllers, Noynoy Aquino, the manipulable son of Cory Aquino, whom the United States had placed in office after the successful "regime change" operation against the last nationalist president of the country, Ferdinand Marcos, in 1986. Obama worked out a deal with the young Aquino, called the Enhanced Defense Cooperation Agreement (EDCA), allowing the deployment of U.S. air, land,

Xinhua/Li Xueren

Philippines President Rodrigo Duterte (left) holds talks China's President, Xi Jinping, in Beijing, Oct. 20, 2016.

and sea military forces into bases across the Philippines, with prepositioning of weapons and military materiel, ready for a war on China. The EDCA agreement was implemented illegally, bypassing the Philippine constitutional requirement for Senate approval for such foreign military deployments on Philippine soil.

Obama then orchestrated a phoney "international tribunal," under the aegis of the Permanent Court of Arbitration at the Hague, which was no tribunal at all, since China refused to participate in the rigged game. The tribunal, composed of anti-China judges chosen by anti-China interests, refused to follow their own guidelines, ruling that China's historical rights have no meaning in the new Alice-in-Wonderland world, but that "international law" is determined by those who pick the judges.

But Obama's dreams of maintaining a unipolar world, with military control over Asia after a probable war with China, have now been dealt a severe blow. Even Wall Street's *Bloomberg News* posted a headline on Oct. 23: "The Philippines Just Blew Up the Obama Pivot."

As you can see in the transcript, Duterte has turned the tables on Obama. While Obama and his "human rights" mafia are denouncing Duterte for the killing of drug dealers in his ferocious war on the drug cartels—cartels that are killing the youth of his country—even demanding that Duterte be taken to the International Criminal Court for "crimes against humanity," Duterte instead indicts the western leaders who have killed hundreds of thousands of innocents in wars against countries which were no threat to the West, from Iraq, to Libya, to Syria today, and even reflecting back on Vietnam, when young Filipino soldiers were also sent to fight and die for a pointless and losing cause in that fellow Southeast Asian nation.

Duterte in China

Duterte's wildly successful trip to China resulted in an agreement to put aside the issues of sovereignty in the South China Sea, and instead to work out agreements for sharing the natural resources in the region and ensuring the peace and stability necessary to deal with the horrific state of the Philippine people and their failed economy. As mentioned in an editorial in China's *Global Times* when Duterte arrived on Oct. 18, 40% of the Philippine people are living in poverty, many of them suffering from hunger. The fishing industry in the Philippines, it said, employs more than 1.6 million people and provides nearly 40% of the protein consumed in the nation. "In this context," it continued, "many Filipinos equate the right to fish as the right to life."

Indeed, one of the most contentious issues between

U.S. Navy/Petty Officer 1st Class Chris Williamson
At Subic Bay, Philippines, Oct. 5, 2016, sailors of the amphibious transport dock ship USS Green Bay participate in the U.S.-Philippine bilateral exercise PHIBLEX.

China and the Philippines has been over fishing rights in the region of the Scarborough Shoal, a contested area between the two countries. When the Aquino government sent Coast Guard boats to push Chinese fishermen out of the area in 2012, the Chinese responded with their own Coast Guard, and have kept Philippipine fishermen out of the region since that time. Now, the two sides are not only working out joint fishing rights, but China has offered to significantly upgrade the fishing industry in the country.

As to the South China Sea, the two sides signed an agreement for the "establishment of a joint coast guard committee on maritime cooperation," while Duterte has announced that there will be no further joint patrols of the region with the United States. On the other hand, the Philippines will become a major part of Xi Jinping's 21st Century Maritime Silk Road, linking the world's maritime nations in win-win development projects.

Altogether, Duterte and the Chinese signed 21 agreements, including $13.5 billion in Chinese soft loans and investments in the Philippines. This includes cooperation in the War on Drugs and investments in rail, roads, agriculture, and more.

ASEAN Unified

Beyond the bilateral agreements, Duterte's rejection of war and confrontation has also facilitated a transformation of the ten-nation Association of Southeast Asian Nations (ASEAN). For years, the Philippines sabotaged the consensus required by the ASEAN Charter, serving as Obama's puppet to demand denunciations of China at ASEAN summits. At the last summit in Laos in September—the first attended by President Duterte—ASEAN came together, expressing its united intent to work with China's Silk Road process, drawing on the China-initiated Asian Infrastructure Investment Bank (AIIB), the Lancang-Mekong Cooperation development plans, and other regional development plans, rejecting confrontation in favor of growth and development.

No to U.S. Policies of War and Poverty

Duterte's dramatic public declaration has been widely publicized in the West. Speaking in the Great Hall of the People in Beijing, he said, "In this venue, I announce my separation from the United States. Not in social matters, but militarily, and in economics also. I have separated from them." Clearly he meant a separation from Obama's war and confrontation *policy* in favor of cooperation with all nations—including the United States, but not in confrontation with others. Economically, he will not reject American investment, but as he makes clear in the transcript below, U.S. investment has been limited to extracting raw materials. The investors have refused to invest a cent in building infrastructure, and that is what the country needs to grow, and which is the core of the offers coming from China.

But Duterte is clearly aware that he has made himself a primary target of the Bush/Obama/British "regime change" imperialism, either by a "color revolution" or by direct assassination or war. His Defense Secretary, Gen. (ret.) Delfin Lorenzana, told the press that in every discussion with his military leaders, Duterte tells them that he may not survive his full term, and that they must continue his uncomprimising war on drugs, crime, terrorism, and subversion.

In the same vein, Duterte's Social Media Director during his presidential campaign, Pompee La Viña, posted on his Facebook page on Oct. 20 an article written by this author in 2004 in *EIR*, describing in detail the coup run by the American neocons in 1986, led by George Shultz, to overthrow President Marcos, in one of the first "color revolutions," making the coup appear to be a "people's power" revolution. In that case the color was yellow. La Viña wrote in his posting (translated from Tagalog): "The Secret Sin of U.S. to Philippines. No secret stays hidden forever. These documents explain how the U.S. IMF "Economic Hitmen" (global elites) helped the "Yellow Oligarchy" take over our country and resources from 1986 to present. Is Uncle Sam our true ally? Think again."[1]

The message is clear. Just as Washington would not allow Marcos to turn the Philippines into a modern nation state—with nuclear power, industrialization, self-sufficiency in food, and friendly relations with China—so it will also try to stop Duterte.

War Danger

Obama is further exposed and weakened by Duterte's courageous moves, but, as Lyndon LaROuche has emphasized, Obama is all the more dangerous, since his last resort is war.

Indeed, Obama's maniacal Defense Secretary "Nuclear Ash" Carter, meeting in Washington with his South Korean counterpart, according to *Voice of America*, declared that "the United States is considering the permanent deployment at its bases in South Korea of B-1B and nuclear-capable B-52 bombers, F-22 Stealth fighter jets, and nuclear-powered submarines." It is widely recognized that such mass overkill, like the deployment of THAAD missiles to South Korea, has no purpose whatsoever against North Korea, but is aimed at China and the Russian Far East.

Stopping such a scenario of doomsday for mankind requires the courage of every citizen of the United States and of the world to stand up against the mad oligarchs in London and Washington, as demonstrated by the "outsider" Duterte, elected President of the Philippines by a population that has finally seen enough of poverty, hunger, drugs, terrorism, and war under U.S. tutelage. The alternative is before us all, in the new paradigm posed by China, Russia, India, and most of the developing nations, who have joined in the "New Silk Road" concept of global development for the common aims of mankind.

mobeir@aol.com

---

1. See Mike Billington, "Shultz and the 'Hit Men' Destroyed the Philippines," *Executive Intelligence Review,* Dec. 24, 2004, p. 20. http://www.larouchepub.com/eiw/public/2004/eirv31n50-20041224/eirv31n50-20041224_020-_shultz_and_the_hit_men_destroyed.pdf/.

The Beijing Press Conference of President of the Philippines Rodrigo Roa Duterte with Foreign Press

At a press conference in Beijing on Oct. 19, Philippine President Rodrigo Duterte delivered this indictment of the war crimes of the British and the Americans over the past century and continuing today. His remarks have been edited and subheads added.

Philippines Government

President Duterte at his press conference in Beijing, Oct. 19.

We've always been allied with the West. In terms of entertainment, education and all, it was all western. As a matter of fact, I am more articulate in talking in English than in my own dialect. Sometimes I have to grope for words. There is one language, Tagalog, which they say is an international dialect, but they have not *perfected* anything. That is why even in the movies, and even in the histories, things were not properly put in place, in the proper perspective. That is even why in the surveys Filipinos placed their trust more with the Americans than the Chinese. During the Cold War, China was portrayed as the bad guy. All of these years, what we read in our books in our schools were all propaganda by those in the West.

I cannot blame the Filipinos for being so indebted, because everything indebted them to the West. Even the reasons for life were placed there, as a war against the Philippines, against the [Japanese] enemies during the second world war. We were hit hard. In the battle of Manila there were 200,000 people killed. The carpet bombings—they were not really made by the Japanese, but by the Americans, to retake the city.

There is no question that in the propaganda, as we grew up, we only read the propaganda of the West. There was the Cold War at the time, and so we could hardly get any news from China and Russia. Those are the realities of life. And so, our foreign policies, up to now, up to this point, were geared toward the people accepted [by the West] in the contending ideologies of the world.

Now that I am President, by the grace of God I read a lot. I am a lawyer, and I study geopolitics and all, and also I am a graduate of the Foreign Service, so I got to know how to balance these contending ideas. I have now the proper perspective to judge whether this foreign policy is good for us or not. I said a few days ago, a few months ago, that I will charter a new course, changing the direction of our foreign policy. I have been friends with everybody, and with no enemies to contend with, no enemies to hurt, no friends to serve.

The War on Drugs

Unfortunately this started with the war against drugs. And I give you the hard numbers. It's four million [addicts] all in all. They are scattered all over the country. There are about six thousand policemen involved it.

What is really very alarming is that my country has already been contaminated with narco politics. I know why you guys are interested in me, because while I was explaining the quandaries of my country and the sheer number and the danger imposed on the next generation, that it will be a failed state, just like in Latin America and even Mexico. On that border between Texas and Mexico, there are about 60,000 deaths. But I never heard of the State Department of Obama and the EU complain about it. They are focusing on me. That issue was already an issue against me when I was Mayor. And they kept hammering on me, criticizing me.

But when I was President—that is something else. Because I represent the country, and if you misrepresent me on the international scene, all the networks here, your networks, and you show it in your own country, it will put shame to my country. And you have something to answer.

Of all the networks, they were only interested in my life, my statement, when I said, internationally, publicly, "If you destroy my country, I will kill you." I was addressing myself to all the drug syndicates, and the drug pushers and all. I said, if you destroy the youth of the land, deprive us of the resources of tomorrow, I will kill you. And it kept on happening, that they said, "The president has been heard saying that he will kill people," because they did not understand the statement, because they were dumb idiots.

You know, China, America, Russia can perfectly say it, and it is very legitimate. "If you kill my country—*if!*" It is conditional! I don't know what has happened to these guys and their grammar. We are not that sophisticated in our English-acquired culture. *If!* So if you do not destroy my country, then I will not kill you! But they kept on hammering on the issues of killing, alone.

They are threatening me with going to the International Criminal Court. I said, that was enough. I said no. Because nobody was listening to me, I gave the word: Bullshit, all of you! Then they suddenly heard, "somebody bullshitting us—who is this guy?" Now they are hearing.

What's wrong with saying I'm going to kill all the criminals? When you are ordering the police — look, the soldiers of my country go to a four year course at the Philippine Military Academy. The police go to the Philippine National Police Academy. They study four years before they become full-fledged law enforcement.

They all know that when you say, "you kill them," it is like in the Old West. It is not our words, it is the words of the American cowboy in the movies! Billy the Kid, wanted, dead or alive! And if you do that in my country, it is not all right. But if they do it in their own country—the funniest thing is it is even at the movies, without the caveat, "warning, this is just movies." Go for them, dead or alive. And when I say I am going to protect my country because I am the President, and I have every right, that is certain. If that is not understood by EU and America, I am sorry for that…. When I said, capture them dead or alive, the policemen and the military know that there has to be some sort of resistance, and that resistance must be violent. Therefore if there is a violent resistance, that is the time that they can use force. If that resistance endangers the life of the police and military, if they believe that they are already in the process of losing their lives, that is the only time they can kill. No need to repeat what they have been taught for four years and has been imbued in their minds. That is the same story for the FBI and the police and everybody….

Why the Change in Foreign Policy?

So, what prompted me to change foreign policy is that the EU signed a manifesto and they told me it was prepared by the lawyers. It said that the lawyers warned me that I can be prosecuted, and then I realized that what is happening now, in the EU, is because they have stupid lawyers. And they can not even agree to let in, let out the migrants. They were so benevolent at first. Now they say, drive them back to the sea, do not accepted them in bondage. So they will die there, and rot in the cold.

Give me a sensible answer. We need to decide here, I will not even have to go to Manila.

America and Britain invaded Iraq, with all the hullabaloo and pronouncements that said "weapons of mass destruction." After killing so many of the soldiers and the republican guards of Saddam—and killed Saddam in the process—they found out, with all its might and technology and human intelligence, that there were no weapons of mass destruction.

If somebody could explain it to me that it was right, stand there in front of me right now, I am willing to listen, and if you do it right, to convince everybody, that after all it was right to invade Iraq, even without the weapons of mass destruction, undermining Libya, wanting to destroy Assad, putting in turmoil Egypt. Now tell me if it is a bright idea of the West, tell me now, justify that it is correct, I will listen and I will resign as the President of the Republic of the Philippines. Was there an explanation? These guys are really convoluted idiots.

You want to prosecute me for what? It is not a crime in my country, especially a President, to warn—or even any President for that matter—"do not do it because I will kill you. Do not enter my boundaries, because if you hurt the people there I will go to war." I just don't know what's happening with the idiots on the other side. My foreign policy goes to where there are people who are sane. Why should I mix my country with very convoluted and almost insane theories of how to run civilization?

Tell me, any one of you—tell me that it was right to invade Iraq, even without the weapons of mass destruction. That was the only thing that kept them going, the weapons of mass destruction. How many died, how many children died in the bombing of Afghanistan? How many died in Vietnam, only to lose it after several decades? And to burn the families there? How many times must this be repeated? Look at Aleppo—when they could have just stopped it, but because earlier they were supplying the arms to the rebels against Syria. But the Chinese government and Russia supported Assad, so you had the longest war there.

So, from where was this ISIS? When was it born? It was born of the desperation of the radicals and rebels of Libya and Syria. That is the beginning of ISIS. America imported terrorism into their territories.

And who was the first to enter the land and took off with the fat of the land, oil? British, American, French, Italians. After so many troubles they partitioned the Middle East, according to tribes, and not of kingdoms. And that is why you have until now fighting amongst themselves. And ISIS became the rallying point. Who imported violence? America. To their lands.

My country, it was occupied by Spain for 400 years. Then it was occupied by the Americans for 50 years. And you think that because that was around a century ago—you should see the pile of bodies where the Moro Muslims of Mindinao, their bodies were dumped there. And they say, "it was 100 years ago, Duterte." No. It still is now.

Why? Because of your convoluted ideas of how to run this civilization.

So, why don't I go to China? What kept us from China was not of our own making. We were almost a vassal state of America. Our foreign policy adopted the policy of the United States and of the West. If they said they hated Russia, we said Amen, and also China. And if they say to go to war in Vietnam, for no reason at all, eventually to lose, we will say, "Yes, we will also send our soldiers there." It is kind of stupid, don't you think?

Nick Ut/Associated Press

"How many died in Vietnam, only to lose [Vietnam] after several decades? And to burn the families there? How many times must this be repeated?"

The Hideous Toll of the Drug Scourge

Now all has been said and done. What gives? Me? Drug war. It is going up to 4 million [drug addicts] now, growing at 700,000 every year. By the end of my term it will reach the 4 million mark. So we will stick with the two-year survey done by General Santiago, a military man of the Drug Enforcement Agency. He said there are already 3 million addicts. Okay.

The mining industry is all over, cutting holes my country, degrading the environment and all. How much does it give my country in taxes? Seventy million U.S. dollars.

There are 3 million Filipinos taking drugs. At one hit per day, that is 6,000 pesos per person per month. If you multiply it by the 3 million, that is 18 billion pesos per month. If you multiply it by 12, that is P216 billion [over $4 billion —ed.] a year. Money, which the father of a family needs to buy rice, medicine, school.

You have girls raped, one-year-olds, two-year-olds, people dying because they were perceived to be devils in front of the addicts. Rape, and even the crime volume, before I was President, puts me to shame.

There are some killed who choose to fight the government. And I said I will have no mercy on you guys. You fight the authorities, you die. It's good for you. You asked for it. I told you before, it will destroy my country. And yet you go in and persist in doing it. And so I said, if you fight, kill them, especially if your life is in danger. Verily I don't want to see military men and policemen die. It should be the bad boys who do the dying. Not my soldiers and police.

So, we're talking about what is right and what is wrong in this world. We're talking of what is moral and what is not. I said I challenge any one of you to come here. We can debate until midnight. Just tell me what was really good when they started to destroy the Middle East. And until now they bomb the hospitals. Patients are dying, and those in the mortuary are dying again. And they go about moralizing the righteousness of the world. I'm sorry. I had to say this.

Why are you veering toward China? Why should I not veer to China? China is good. It has never invaded a piece of my country all these generations. All they want is to do business, barter trade, even before the arrival of the Spaniards. There are a lot of Chinese-descent Filipinos. Almost every one. We have not seen any wars or atrocities committed of late. There were wars with Genghis Khan and Kublai Khan—that is another thing, for the history books.

Obama Steps Up War Provocations Against Russia

by Carl Osgood

Oct. 24—The surreal *opera bouffe* which is now playing out within the United States, known as the U.S. Presidential campaign, has been unsuccessful in obscuring the reality of an intensifying world crisis, a crisis deepening and worsening day-by-day. Over the recent weeks the world has witnessed a chain of events and actions which are leading toward open military conflict between the United States and Russia. The mad dog Obama Administration, striking out in several different directions simultaneously, has taken one provocative step after another, each one heightening the potential for war to erupt.

On October 22, 2016, in a discussion with associates, Lyndon LaRouche assessed the current status of Obama's intentions in the following way:

Obama probably would like to destroy everything. But perhaps at the same time, he does not think that he has the power, or his advisors suggest that he does not have the power to make an open move. Or, is he doing a surprise attack by going at a point of attack which other people are not likely to foresee. Those are the issues. A possible, crucial demonstration of action...

Only one thing is really clear on this matter. If they're trying to pretend not to start war because Obama and the British, in particular, are aware of their military weakness,

President Barack Obama

The White House

and therefore, are they going with a special kind of operation, hoping they can pull a stunt which they could not pull in terms of a normal way of getting into warfare. That's what the issue is...

We have to get to the characteristic which suggests that either Obama's ready to go, or he's cowardly. Unless you can determine those things, you don't have a strategic insight. You have to find out the nature of the condition: Are they actually doing things which indicate that they're moving to potential warfare, or are they just making noises, because that's the problem. And this involves the general idea of traps, military traps...

The question is to what degree and in what form is such a potential in place. What it is or is not acting, or seems not to be acting when it might be acting: that's what you have to look for.

Let's look it from that standpoint. Obama's in a tough situation on his side. But he's still acting. The British system and so forth are still doing these things; they have not quit. Now, if they have not quit, that means they have not surrendered. If they have not surrendered, then the war is on.

Obama Acts

Events over the recent days cohere exactly with this analysis by Mr. LaRouche. In particular, since the time of the September 9 agreement between U.S. Secretary of State John Kerry and Russian Foreign Minister Sergei Lavrov on a cease fire in Aleppo, Syria, the Obama Administration has embarked on a course of events that is greatly intensifying the danger of war with Russia at the strategic level. The Obama Administration's sabotage of the Kerry/Lavrov agreement, only days after it went into effect, has been followed by unprecedented nuclear saber rattling by U.S. Secretary of Defense Ash Carter as well as threats by Vice President Joe Biden to carry out massive cyber attacks on Russia.

CC/Kelly Kline

Vice President Joseph Biden

Vice President Biden, in an interview with NBC's "Meet the Press" that was taped on Oct. 14, issued a threat of cyber warfare against Moscow, stating that this would "send a message" to Russian President Vladimir Putin. "He'll know it," Mr. Biden said. "And it will be at the time of our choosing. And under the circumstances that have the greatest impact." Shortly after the Biden statements were first aired, NBC News reported that the White House has tasked the CIA with developing "options" for a wide-ranging "clandestine" cyber operation designed to harass and "embarrass" the Kremlin leadership. According to the NBC reporter, however, there is doubt among some officials within the Obama Administration of whether or not such a scheme would work or even if Putin is "embarrassable."

Biden's threats followed

YouTube

Director of National Intelligence James Clapper

the Oct. 7 joint statement by Director of National Intelligence James Clapper and Secretary of Homeland Security Jeh Johnson, in which they asserted that the Russian Government had conducted cyber attacks on U.S. election systems, including servers and email systems of the Democratic Party. The Russians, they claim, had then leaked the content of these emails to Wikileaks and DCleaks.com. Not one shred of evidence has been presented by anyone in the Obama Administration to support these accusations. Instead, Clapper and Johnson assert that the leaks are "consistent with the methods and motivations of Russian-directed efforts," and "are intended to interfere with the U.S. election process." However, one intelligence expert pointed out to *EIR* on Oct. 20 that the use of the word "confident" in the Clapper-Johnson statement indicates that no real evidence exists and that there is widespread disagreement in the intelligence community about who was actually responsible for the hacks.

This has not prevented the White House from issuing the threat, however. The fact that it was Biden who delivered the threat, on national television, no less, rather than anonymous U.S. sources in print, indicates that the theat comes from Barack Obama, himself.

Russian officials responded sharply to Biden's cyberwar threat. Russia Channel One featured the Biden threat as the second lead news item after the BRICS summit, reporting that "Moscow took sharp notice of the fact that this threat was voiced at such a high political level. In the U.S.A., by the way, after Biden's statement, the media started reporting that some kind of overall answer to Russia is in preparation. What it might be, no one knows. Recently at the State Department there was talk about Russia losing more planes in Syria and sending its servicemen home in body-bags."

President Vladimir Putin's spokesman Dmitry Peskov issued a statement Oct. 16, declaring, "The fact is, U.S. unpredictability and aggression keep growing, and such threats against Moscow and our country's leadership are unprecedented, because the threat is being announced at the level of the U.S. Vice President. Of course, given such an aggressive, unpredictable line, we have to take measures to protect our interests; somehow hedge the risks. *Such unpredictability is dangerous for the whole world.*"

Konstantin Kosachov, the head of the Federation Council (upper house) Committee on International Affairs, told Russia Channel One's prime time "Vremya" news program that "This is a direct threat of the use of force by the U.S.A.; an unprecedented event. There has been nothing like this since the Cuban Missile Crisis of 1962. This is a threat of cyber terrorism, coming from a state. It is an emergency, which should be taken up at the level of the UNSC, and which requires Russia to take all possible measures to insure its national security."

Nuclear Threats

On September 26, U.S. Defense Secretary Ash Carter traveled to Minot AFB in North Dakota, where, with a B-52 bomber parked behind him, he delivered a speech on U.S. nuclear deterrence and the importance of providing "options" to the President should deterrence fail. Biden asserted that the landscape has changed over the last 25 years, saying, "One way the nuclear landscape has changed: we didn't build new types of nuclear weapons or delivery systems for the last 25

DoD/U.S. Navy Petty Officer 1st Class Chad J. McNeeley

Secretary of Defense Ashton Carter at Panmunjom, in the demilitarized zone between North and South Korea.

years, but others did, at the same time that our allies in Asia, the Middle East, and NATO did not... so we must continue to sustain our deterrence." On Russia, he claimed "there is some doubt about Russian leaders' strategies for the weapons." He expressly called out Russia for its "recent nuclear saber-rattling" that "raises serious questions" about Moscow's commitment to the global post-Cold War nuclear posture. India and China, on the other hand, "are behaving responsibly with their nuclear enterprises."

Carter continued, "Even in 2016, deterrence still depends on perception what potential adversaries see, and therefore believe about our will and ability to act. This means that as their perceptions shift, so must our strategy and actions." A large-scale nuclear attack is not likely, the secretary said. The most likely scenario is "the unwise resort to smaller but still unprecedentedly terrible attacks, for example by Russia or North Korea, to try to coerce a conventionally superior opponent to back off or abandon an ally during a crisis. We cannot allow that to happen, which is why we're working with our allies in both regions to innovate and operate in new ways that sustain deterrence and continue to preserve strategic stability."

Therefore, according to Carter/Obama, the replacement of the entire U.S. nuclear delivery system is required, all of it, not parts of it, as some have argued, but every bit of it. "If we don't replace these systems, quite simply they will age even more, and become unsafe, unreliable, and ineffective," Carter said. And, if some parts of it are lost, "That would mean losing confidence in our ability to deter, which we can't afford in today's volatile security environment."

In truth, Carter's statements are worthy of the Joseph Goebbels, who, in 1939, proclaimed that the Nazi blitz-krieg against Poland was a "defensive" action to protect Germany against Polish military threats. It was the United States, under George W. Bush in 2002, who uni-laterally abrogated the Anti-Ballistic Missile (ABM) treaty, thus setting into motion the current arms build-up. It is the United States, under both Bush and Obama, which has pursued an aggressive policy of NATO mili-tary expansion into Easten Europe, right up to the bor-ders of Russia. It was the United States, under Obama, which sponsored the 2014 Ukraine coup d'etat against the constitutionally elected government of the Ukraine, for the purpose of bringing the Ukraine into NATO and establishing a NATO naval base in Crimea. And it is the United States today which is arming and supporting the terrorist armed forces in Syria and threatening to impose a no-fly zone to protect those terrorists, a no-fly zone which could lead directly to U.S.-Russian armed clashes.

All of Russia's current actions must be placed within the context of the war threat coming from the Obama Administration and NATO. This is the case with Russian President Vladimir Putin's decree, just approved by the State Duma this week, suspending the U.S.-Russia plutonium disposal treaty. The Russians have specifically cited the deterioration in U.S.-Rus-sian relations, a deterioration largely the result of U.S. actions, as a significant factor, alongside inadequate compliance by the U.S., in the decision to suspend the treaty.

In a direct response to Ash Carter's Minot speech, the Russian Foreign Ministry issued a reply on Septem-ber 29, saying that Russia will have to take into account U.S. approaches on nuclear deterrence and take counter measures to ensure its national security. That reply stated, "Carter's statement means that if Russia comes under attack from U.S. allies, the Americans will be ready to back it and threaten to use their nuclear weap-ons against us. We would like to think that Washington understands the meaning of such statements and their possible consequences for international security and stability.

"It is not only their over-the-top Russophobia, which has unfortunately become of late a norm for public speeches by representatives of the outgoing ad-ministration," the ministry said, but there is also a "se-rious concern over the mentioned readiness to use their nuclear potentials in case of an armed conflict with Russia, with an aim to prevent our country from a pos-sibility to use nuclear weapons to rebuff aggression [i.e. a strategic doctrine to pre-emptively knock out any Russian "second strike" potential]... Of course we will have to keep in mind U.S. approaches and take necessary counter measures to ensure our national se-curity.

"We note that the Pentagon chief's belligerent rhet-oric helps to a large extent clarify the real goals behind the ongoing modernization of the U.S. nuclear weap-ons," the Russian Foreign Ministry said. "The strategy of pressuring Russia by force, which in the logic of its Pentagon 'planners' apparently means nuclear brink-manship, will receive a more sophisticated and danger-ous military-technical foundation."

While Carter was issuing his nuclear threat, the Obama Administration was preparing to ramp up its dispute with Russia over the Intermediate-Range Nu-clear Forces (INF) Treaty. Through unnamed officials and members of the U.S. Congress, the Obama admin-istration unleashed a new torrent of accusations against Russia for alleged violations of the INF Treaty, via the *New York Times* on October 19. "Russia appears to be moving ahead with a program to produce a ground-launched cruise missile, despite the Obama administra-tion's protests that the weapon violates a landmark arms control agreement," wrote the *Times*' Michael Gordon. "American officials are now expressing concerns that Russia is producing more missiles than are needed to sustain a flight-test program, spurring fears that the Kremlin is moving to build a force that could ultimately be deployed."

Escalating the pressure against Russia, the Obama Administration has called a meeting of the Special Ver-ification Commission, the body set up by the treaty to deal with verification issues, despite the fact that the Commission hasn't met since 2003.

Rep. Mac Thornberry (R-Tex.), chairman of the House Armed Services Committee, and Rep. Devin Nunes (R-Calif.), the chairman of the House Intelli-

Russian Deputy Foreign Minister Sergei Ryabkov: "There will be no more 7-day truces, because they allow the jihadis to regroup and rearm." Here, a Russian Su-34 conducting an airstrike in Syria

gence Committee, have jumped on board the Obama war-confrontation drive. In an October 17 letter, they called on Obama to "confront Russia's violation" of the treaty. "The United States must finally impose penalties for Russia's near decade long pattern of violations that undermine this seminal arms control treaty and place it on the verge of collapse," they write. "It has now become apparent to U.S. that the situation regarding Russia's violation has worsened and Russia is now in material breach of the treaty," and the U.S. must act accordingly."

Syria Threats

The September 9 Kerry-Lavrov agreement, according to the text that was later leaked by the Associated Press, called for the separation of the U.S.-backed opposition groups from Jabhat Fateh al Sham, the group that was formerly known as the Al Qaeda-affiliated Jabhat al Nusra. The group had changed its name and formally broke with Al Qaeda in July, as a way of increasing the confusion on the ground as to who is a terrorist and who is a "moderate." Nonetheless, for a few days, at least, after the Kerry-Lavrov agreement was announced, the Obama Administration gave the appearance of joining with Russia to fight terrorists in Syria. That was blown apart, however, when U.S. and Danish warplanes bombed Syrian army positions on hilltops outside of Deir Ezzor on September 17, killing at least 62 to 82 Syrian soldiers and wounding about 100 more. U.S. Central Command alleged in a statement that the bombing was an accident and lied outright that the U.S. military had informed the Russian command in Syria that the U.S. would be carrying out air strikes in that area. When Russia called an emergency U.N. Security Meeting that evening to discuss the U.S. attack, the Obama Administration's U.N. ambassador, Samantha Power, went ballistic

Two days later, a UN/Red Crescent humanitarian aid convoy in southwestern Aleppo province was attacked and burned, destroying 18 of the 31 trucks and killing about 20 aid workers. The U.S. immediately blamed Russia, even though, as the Russian Defense Ministry pointed out, images of the aid convoy didn't show the kind of damage consistent with air-dropped, high explosive munitions. Following that attack, the U.S. and UK governments, with no evidence whatsoever to support their claims, launched an intense campaign to accuse Russia of committing war crimes in Syria, threatening to take Russia to the International Criminal Court, as well as a "plan B" military response to "stop the massacre of civilians."

State Department spokesman John Kirby went so far as to issue a threat against Russia, one noted by many Russian officials, saying to reporters, on September 28, that the consequences of Russia not obeying America's diktats in Syria "are that the civil war will continue in Syria, that extremists and extremists groups will continue to exploit the vacuums that are there in Syria to expand their operations, which will include, no question, attacks against Russian interests, perhaps even Russian cities, and Russia will continue to send troops home in body bags, and they will continue to lose resources—even, perhaps, more aircraft. The stability that they claim they seek in Syria will be ever more elusive…" Any illusion that the U.S. was aligning with Russia to fight terrorism in Syria was demolished by that statement, replaced by intense war propaganda from the Obama Administration and statements from Moscow that the U.S. was actually aligned, now, with the terrorist groups.

At the Russian Foreign Ministry, Deputy Foreign Minister Sergei Ryabkov was uncompromising. There will be no more 7-day truces, because they allow the jihadis to regroup and rearm, he said, and the failure of the diplomatic track "is going on due to Washington's inability to fulfill its obligations and promises," and is therefore on the conscience of decisions made by the U.S. "We are outraged at the ultimatum-like tone of the signals that we are getting. Sometimes we even hear cynical threats against us and those who are really fighting terrorists in Syria. We can't consider it anything else but de-facto support of terrorists by the U.S." Ryabkov called Washington's threats "an emotional breakdown amid the inability of the Obama administration to implement its part of the agreements" on Syria. "The U.S. is in fact bringing grist to the terrorists' mill providing them with undisguised support."

The Russian Foreign Ministry, in an October 3 statement, effectively charged Obama with being in league with the same terrorists who brought down the World Trade Center towers on September 11, 2001. "In conditions when all seem to recognize that in question is a terrorist organization having direct links with Al Qaeda which committed terrific terrorist attacks in the United States 15 years ago, the Barack Obama administration is in no hurry to separate anti-government groups oriented towards Washington from it," the ministry said. "On the contrary, it shields it by opposition groups that have formally declared their commitment to the cease-fire regime but in fact merged into it."

The "plan B" military options, according to numerous news reports through the month of October, include a no fly zone over Aleppo and/or a safe zone in northern Syria, air or cruise missile strikes against Syrian air force bases, supplying the Western-Gulf

DoD photo/Cherie Cullen
U.S. Army Gen. David Petraeus

states-backed jihadi opposition groups with heavier weapons, including shoulder-fired anti-aircraft missiles. Publicly, Hillary Clinton and many of her supporters in the neo-con war party are calling for the establishment of an aggressive no-fly zone over parts of Syria, the parts where the Russian air contingent is active, along with the Syrian air force. Retired General and former CIA director David Petraeus told PBS host Charlie Rose on September 29 that he thought it was "not too late" to set up a no-fly zone. "It's not too late to declare a safe zone. And it's not too late to declare a no-fly zone. And indeed if the regime air force, for example, bombs folks we're supporting or we're concerned about, we tell them we're going to ground your air force," Petraeus said. During the third presidential debate on October 19, Clinton defended the idea, claiming that "A no-fly zone can save lives and hasten the end of the conflict," adding that a larger war could be avoided with proper planning. Neither she nor Petraeus really addressed the question of what should be done should Russian planes challenged a U.S.-imposed no fly zone.

In London, the answer to that question is simply: Shoot them down. Andrew Mitchell, a Tory member of Parliament and a former development secretary, told an emergency session of the House of Commons on October 11 that Western air forces must be willing to confront Russian military jets over the skies of Syria to enforce a no-fly zone. Incredibly, Mitchell likened the Russian attacks on the terrorist forces in Aleppo with the fascist bombardment of Guernica during the Spanish civil war. "What we are saying is very clear. No one wants to see a firefight with Russia, no one wants to shoot down a Russian plane," Mitchell told BBC Radio 4. "But what we do say is that the international community has an avowed responsibility to protect, and that protection must be exerted. If that means confronting Russian air power defensively, on behalf of the innocent people on the ground who we are trying to protect,

In Syria, members of the Al-Nusra Front, another name for Al Qaeda, claims of separation notwithstanding.

VoA

allies, including the main European countries. ... Remember what Libya or Iraq looked like before these countries and their organizations were destroyed as states by our Western partners' forces?" Prior to the Western military interventions, "these states showed no signs of terrorism. They were not a threat for Paris, for the Cote d'Azur, for Belgium, for Russia, or for the United States," Putin pointed out. "Now, they are the source of terrorist threats. Our goal is to prevent the same from happening in Syria."

When asked why Russian planes were not bombing ISIS instead of Aleppo, he said: "It is another terrorist group, Jabhat al-Nusra, that controls the situation in Aleppo. This group was always considered a wing of Al Qaeda and is included in the UN's list of terrorist organizations. What we find particularly depressing and hard to understand is that our partners, especially the Americans, are always finding a way to try to exclude this group from the list of terrorist organizations. ... They want to use these terrorist organizations' and radicals' combat potential to pursue their own political aims, in this case, to combat President Assad and his government, and do not understand that they cannot simply stall them [the rebels] and get them to live by civilized rules after they have tasted victory over someone."

As for humanitarian access to Aleppo, Putin said that everyone agrees on this. Everyone agrees that the Syrian army should pull back from the side of the road that it occupies, and the militants should pull back from the other side. "They either do not want to or cannot pull the militants back," he said. "It has been proposed that our armed units, Russian military personnel, be deployed on the road to ensure transit safety. The Russian military, who are courageous and decisive people, have said they would do it," he went on. "But I told them that this could only be done jointly with the U.S., and ordered them to make the proposal. We have proposed this, and they [the Americans] promptly refused. They do not want to deploy their troops there, but they also do not want to pull these opposition groups back, who are really terrorists. What can we do in this situation?"

then we should do that." David Petraeus, according to the London *Guardian,* is among Mitchell's military advisors on the no-fly zone question.

Also under consideration, according to a report in the October 23 *Washington Post,* is a plan, by the Obama Administration, to supply U.S.-backed armed terrorist groups with heavier weapons, to be used against both the legitimate Syrian government and Russian military forces.

Putin Responds

In an interview with French TF-1 television, recorded on October 12, Putin refuted the accusations coming from Europe and the U.S. that Russia is committing war crimes in Syria, and he succinctly explained why Russia is in Syria. The war crimes charges are "political rhetoric that does not have great significance and does not take into account the real situation in Syria," he said. "I believe deeply that some of the responsibility for what is happening in the region in general and in Syria in particular lies especially with our Western partners, above all the U.S.A. and its

ON THE FIFTH ANNIVERSARY OF
THE ASSASSINATION OF QADDAFI, WE DECLARE:

A Vote for Barack Obama Is a Vote For Thermonuclear War!

Remove Him Now!

Oct. 25—It was five years ago that Lyndon LaRouche, alone, declared that the assassination of Qaddafi was the beginning of war with Russia. In his October 28, 2011 statement, "Qaddafi's Death," LaRouche said:

The manner in which British-directed interests, acting in concert with the British puppet known as U.S. President Barack Obama, have created and manipulated the recent warfare within Libya, has now created a serious, more or less immediate threat-potential of a "Third World War." This is a threat potential which is coincident with the immediately threatened, general breakdown-crisis of the already hyper-bankrupt,

trans-Atlantic monetarist system. That is to emphasize, that the manner in which the British-directed alliance in the Libya affair has concluded the Libya crisis, has turned the Libya affair itself into the threatened role of a detonator of the potential world-warfare which has been accumulated in the Southwest Asian "cockpit." British-centered imperialist interests, as typified by the role of former Prime Minister Tony Blair as a featured instrument, using U.S. President Barack Obama as their puppet, have now created a pregnant state of world affairs akin to that portrayed in a virtual new H.G. Wells fantasy under the theme of "world warfare"—a

quivering potential of a "third world war." The Anglo-Saudi orchestration of the September 11, 2001 attack on the United States, has been a crucial element in preparing the way for the threat which came to the surface of current strategic developments with the manner of the murder of the Qaddafi party.

Killing Qaddafi

Obama's deployment to kill Qaddafi was merely to perform the role of a "closer" in the conclusion of a British imperial policy personally carried out by Tony Blair and Jacob (and later Nathan) Rothschild, who became members of the board of Qaddafi's $100 billion Libyan Investment Authority in 2007. Seven months before Qaddafi's 2011 assassination, Jeff Steinberg reported in *EIR* that:

> In March 2004, six months after the UN sanctions were lifted, Blair was the first Western head of state, since the 1988 Pan Am 103 bombing, to travel to Libya and meet with Qaddafi. In the aftermath of the Blair trip, a British-Libyan Business Council was established to open the economic spigot from Qaddafi to the City of London... In 2007, Blair made his second trip to Libya as Prime Minister... At this time, Blair ally and Inter-Alpha Group founder Lord Jacob Rothschild was put on the board of the Libyan Investment Authority (LIA), Qaddafi's $100 billion sovereign wealth fund. Once he left office as prime minister, Blair, too, joined the board of LIA.
>
> By the time that Lord Jacob "retired" from the LIA board in 2009, his son Nathaniel "Nat" Rothschild had moved into the Libyan franchise, cultivating a close personal relationship with Qaddafi's son, Saif al-Islam Qaddafi.

Consider, for a moment, Blair's actual role in the instigation of the criminal and illegal Iraq War of 2003, a role for which he merits prosecution for international war crimes committed against humanity—well over a million people in fact. Consider, also, Prime Minister Blair's role in the death of David Kelly, who attempted to expose the fraudulent nature of the entire Iraq adventure. Though Qaddafi did not realize it, with Blair and Rothschild's board appointments, the "Order of the Assassins" had moved into place, sitting directly opposite to Qaddafi in the closed sessions of his Libyan Investment Authority.

Qaddafi's murder was planned and carried out with the same malice aforethought as that of Julius Caesar, but with the dirty work left to the United States. Obama's personal execution of Qaddafi was savored as a television entertainment by Obama: he had his staff, including Hilary Clinton, join him for the festivities. "We came, we saw, he died," was Clinton's accurate, infamous statement about that lethal "Roman Coliseum" broadcast.

The dismemberment of Libya was done as part of the scorched-earth policy of the Obama Administration toward Libya, Chad, Niger and other African nations, as well as the rest of the world. His is a generalized depopulation strategy intended to counter China's growing and positive world economic influence; Russia's indispensable leadership role in Syria, Iran, and with the BRICS nations; and the emerging dialogue of scientific optimism that is on the verge of producing a cultural renaissance worldwide, in the form of joint space exploration and joint space missions among former adversaries. Obama's bankrupt "desert pharaoh" policy, to the contrary, is to scorch the globe in pursuit of the imperial objectives of the British Empire. The preferred weapons of Obama's Apocalypse are a combination of trans-Atlantic monetary chaos and financial collapse, with what is sometimes euphemistically referred to as the "Revolution in Military Affairs," a "revolution" whose moral content is captured in Obama's Nero-like Tuesday drone-killing ritual murders.

The Revolution in Military Affairs (RMA) was once declared by Duke University's Triangle Institute for Security Studies director Peter Feaver to in fact be "neo-feudalism": "In fact, what we're seeing is a return to neo-feudalism. If you think about how the East India Company played a role in the rise of the British Empire, there are similar parallels to the rise of the American quasi-empire." Financiers George Shultz and Felix Rohaytn are two American "old boy mechanics" deployed by British and continental European oligarchical "old money" on behalf of this outlook. The goal is to privatize killing by authorizing non-governmental private armies to be deployed through "public-private partnerships" in the form of death and extermination squads.

Obama: British Agent

For the past quarter century, since the 1991 collapse of the Soviet Union, the mad dream of an Anglo-American "unipolar world," ruled under the umbrella of the "Five Eyes"—Britain, Canada, Australia, New Zealand and a royally sodomized United States—had been the underlying motive for many different schemes. They are called by many names—"Project for a New American Century," "NAFTA," the "Trans-Pacific Partnership"—but they are all the same. Their origin is less well known.

Barack Obama's job, for which he was selected to serve two terms as the American President, is to re-attach the United States to the British Empire from the which it bloodily broke two and a half centuries ago. His conflict with Vladimir Putin, the which Obama himself may not even fully understand, must risk nuclear war in order that the cultural and economic upshift that the collaboration of Russia and China could represent for the world, not re-infect the United States itself. The British have never forgiven Benjamin Franklin, George Washington and Alexander Hamilton for what America threatened to do to the British Empire, but has so far failed to finish. It is America which is seen as the primary enemy of the British, not Russia or China; Hamilton's ideas are the true basis for eliminating the existence of the imperial world order once and for all. It is this latter existential threat to the financial predators that most worries them about the continued existence of Lyndon LaRouche, his movement, and his forecasting capability in a time of the luridly public incompetence of the "financial and political elites."

Obama's drone war and use of drones, is already being turned into "the next big thing" by his financial angel and first campaign manager, Union Bank of Switzerland's (UBS) Robert Wolf. *Bloomberg News*, in "A Top Fundraiser for Obama Turns From Wall Street to Drones" on April 29, 2015, reported:

> Wearing cuff links with the U.S. presidential seal, Robert Wolf was explaining why he loves drones and wants to help big companies fly them... "I've been in business for 30 years—this is the most exciting thing I've ever done," said Wolf, who left UBS during Obama's 2012 re-election campaign to start 32 Advisors, which also offers economic advice, brokers infrastructure deals and helps foreign governments get investments. "Just to be clear, this is going to change the landscape."

Look at the role of the same Robert Wolf in the organizing of the Obama campaign. Before Obama had even announced his bid for President, the UBS's Wolf took over and designed what would become Obama's Presidential campaign in the fall of 2006, after a meeting between Obama and George Soros in New York City. The "little people small contributions fundraising" for Obama was a myth. Obama's campaign was a Wall Street/City of London continuation of the Bush Presidency. It was a "breakthrough Presidential campaign," but in a completely different sense. His Administration has succeeded only in droning the innocent, protecting Wall Street, and advancing Cecil Rhodes' goal of the reincorporation of the United States into the British Empire.

Remove Obama Now!

The Russians and Chinese had been assured by the Obama Administration that the Libyan campaign was not intended to topple and assassinate Qaddafi. Obama lied to them. In December of 2011, Putin, during a four and a half hour exchange with press, said about the killing of Qaddafi: "Who did this? Drones, including American ones. They attacked his column. Then—through the special forces, who should not have been there—they brought in the so-called opposition and fighters, and killed him without court or investigation." Putin will not allow the same mistake to be made in Syria, and in his campaign there has baffled, frustrated and thwarted Obama at every turn. At the same time, he has made it clear that he will welcome any sincere effort to dismantle the terrorist capabilities that have been so strengthened by the fall of Libya and by the creation and maintenance of ISIS. He will also not allow the overthrow of the Assad regime desired by Obama to result in the creation of a generalized zone of instability and continuous crisis, a condition which at some point will lead to an undesired but inevitable confrontation with Israel—and, perhaps, its thermonuclear arsenal.

Vladimir Putin, not Barack Obama, is the sane force on the world stage today. Obama's sanity is severely questionable. For example, Obama says he regards the 2016 Presidential election as a referendum on his personal Presidential legacy. The only clear legacy Obama has, is his Tuesday execution sessions. Obama is clearly mentally unbalanced, a thermonuclear Nero. Use the Twenty- Fifth amendment now against Obama, and the most dangerous possibility—the possibility that the five year process that began with Qaddafi's criminal execution will conclude in general thermonuclear war—will be removed as well.

Don't degrade yourself any longer. Vote for principle. Remove Obama now.

www.ingramcontent.com/pod-product-compliance
Lightning Source LLC
Chambersburg PA
CBHW051950280526
45789CB00009B/3247